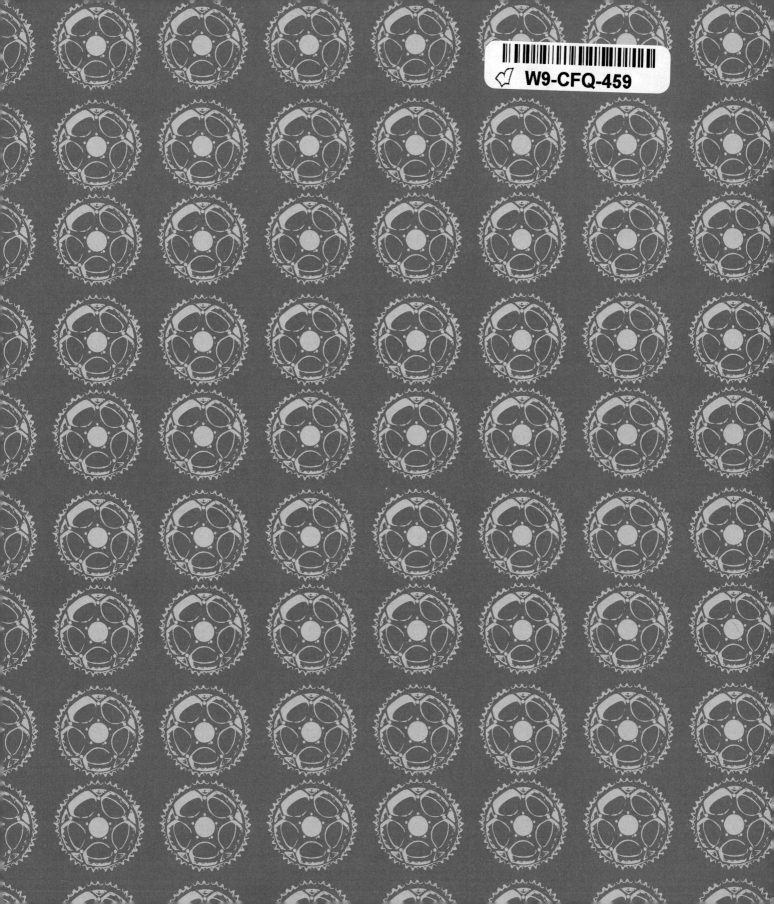

FAT TIRE

A celebration of the mountain bike
by Amici Design

CHRONICLE BOOKS

SAN FRANCISCO

Schwinn Bicycles advertisement on page 22, from the book *Schwinn Bicycles*
by Jay Pridmore and Jim Hurd, copyright © 1996, used by permission of MBI Publishing Company.

Library of Congress Cataloging-in-Publication Data:

Fat Tire: A Celebration of the Mountain Bike / by Amici Design.
p. cm.
ISBN 0-8118-1982-5
1. All terrain cycling. I. Amici Design (firm)
GV1056.F38 1999
796.6'3–dc21   98-4094
                              CIP

Manufactured in China

Cover design: Amici Design

Director/Designer: Lee Jakobs
Editor: Dan Imhoff
Art Director: Roberto Carra
Contributing Writers: Dan Imhoff,
Dan Koeppel, Joe Breeze,
Mark Reidy, Jenny Fenster

Distributed in Canada by Raincoast Books,
8680 Cambie Street
Vancouver, BC V6P 6M9

10 9 8 7 6 5 4 3 2 1

Chronicle Books
85 Second Street
San Francisco, CA 94105

www.chroniclebooks.com

Acknowledgments

Amici Design cannot begin to thank all those contributors who helped put this book together, but we'll try, and please forgive us if we've inadvertently forgotten anyone. First and foremost we thank Michael Carabetta and Christina Wilson at Chronicle Books. Secondly, all those who contributed editorial assistance, including Joe Breeze, Connie Thorpe, Dan Koeppel, Jenny Fenster, Frank Berto, Paolo Salvagione, Charlie Kelly, Gary Fisher, and Chris Jorgensen. Thirdly, Tom Larter at Giro, Tim Parr at Swobo, Chris Zigmont at Mavic, Steve Boehmke at Shimano, Lori Epsen at Specialized, and Elayna Caldwell at RockShox, and all the other manufacturers as well as Mill Valley Cycle Works for their generous contributions. And lastly, Kay Peterson-Cook from the Mountain Bike Hall of Fame.

A big thanks as well to all of the contributing photographers who maintain their living by traveling the world capturing exceptional photos for us to see in publications and books. It is their appreciation and love for the sport of mountain biking that helped make this project possible. Contact and photo credits can be found on page 142.

We were just havin' fun ...

 I remember sitting on my 1937 Schwinn atop Mt. Tamalpais with riding buddy Otis Guy in the mid-1970s. Both of us were spattered head to toe with mud, and as I looked out over the San Francisco Bay Area I said to him, "This sure is a whole lot of fun, but who else would want to do it?"

The tremendous worldwide popularity of the mountain bike today might lead one to believe that its creation was obvious. But it didn't begin with one person exclaiming, "Here it is—the bike of the future!" followed by a clamor to copy it and reap profits. That came later.

An oft-quoted line from Marin County mountain-biking lore goes, "Heck, we were just havin' fun." Or were we? Don't get me wrong, we *were* having fun—and loads of it. But mountain biking happened because it was the next evolutionary step for bicycling in the grander scheme of things, *and* because it was fun. If we had just been seeking fun, we probably would've followed the next craze to come along, but we found some innate staying power with bicycles.

None of us realized the influence that the Marin off-road scene would eventually have on cycling and on our culture. We hadn't a clue whether our fascination with fat tire bikes was going to be just another in a series of isolated occurrences around the nation (there had been many of these since fat tires existed), or if it would grow beyond our immediate area. The seed needed pollination. It took the right place and time, and most importantly, hundreds of cyclists, for the sport to take hold. Why did it happen here? What may have been the deciding factor was simply where we were.

It's no revelation that California has a reputation for maverick ideas. Our population consists of, in a general sense, dreamers; I suppose it's in our DNA. California's abundant natural wealth has long drawn dream-chasers from around the globe, such as those who poured into San Francisco in 1849. Their gold-rush legacy is still unmistakably with us. We are, as a whole, a little more receptive to new ideas, and perhaps vulnerable to grand schemes as well.

The San Francisco Bay region's beauty also played a role by attracting lovers of the outdoors. There has been a strong outdoor-oriented community here for over a hundred years, a love passed down to succeeding generations. For many Marin County families, life involves a 2,600-foot-high backyard called Mt. Tamalpais. My parents had me climbing to the top of Tam from the age of five.

Naturally, with such outdoor beauty comes a desire to protect it. The 1960s saw the biggest conservation movement in this country since the 1890s, an awareness that culminated in the first Earth Day in 1970. Perhaps the single most important impetus to cycling, however, was a percolating interest in physical fitness to counter the sedentary American lifestyle. This started in the 1950s, when President Eisenhower's doctor put him on a bike to help him recover from a heart attack. My generation was the first to grow up with the encouragement from the Presidential Physical Fitness Awards, which existed right through the Carter administration. Bikes offered us exercise and mobility for adventure.

By the early 1970s, a bike boom was in full swing across the country. Riders' rights organizers had taken to the streets and racers had taken to the peleton. Marin had one of the highest densities of cyclists. The bicycle, which Americans had viewed for most of this century as merely a child's toy, was gaining recognition as the most efficient method of personal transport, and a sustainable one at that. The Mideast oil crisis and the gasoline price shocks of 1974 and 1978 helped. The popular bike at the time was the ten-speed, a skinny tire, drop-handlebar road-racer. This was not necessarily the best bike for the job, and certainly not a bike for the average person.

In 1972, a group of us formed Marin's Velo Club Tamalpais, an alternative racing club that grew to about a hundred members and became our extended family. Some of us reached the highest level in U.S. road racing. Training 250 to 400 miles a week, we intimately knew all the local roads in a 75-mile radius.

At the same time, many of us were rediscovering old balloon-tire bikes in junkyards and old bike shops. These "clunkers" were the alter egos of our refined road racers, and we'd take them up on the trails of Tam. While the hilly, twisty roads in our area were certainly scenic and challenging, the off-road experience was an intensely distilled version of it all. We doubled our riding territory and tripled our fun.

Despite the ubiquitous fun, it was the bicycle's individual and societal implications of health that gave our young mountain bike movement its grip. The bike's inherent usefulness was the glue that held it all together, that kept it alive, until the sport was born at the watershed race called Repack in 1976 and swept across the nation to a receptive audience.

For all those people who had previously walked down a trail and seen the sign "Hot Springs, 20 miles" and wished they could get there that day, suddenly there was a way. For all those people who had walked into a bike shop and hadn't seen a bike that looked practical, now there was an option. I remember that, in the 1970s, noncycling buddies would take a look at my old Schwinn Excelsior or my custom-made Breezer and say, "That's an interesting bike. Mind if I try it?" And invariably they would ride back with a huge grin and exclaim, "Where has this bike been?!" They loved it. I think this was when I realized we were on to something that was more than just fun in the hills. Here was the bike of dreams, the bike that made bikes relevant. It was comfortable, easy to use, useful, and fun; a bike for street and trail.

From the first days of Repack, racing—in both the competition and the technological innovation it engendered—became a driving force in the sport's meteoric growth. This has been aided by a self-sufficiency clause in the National Off-Road Bicycling Association (NORBA) charter that requires racers to fix all their own mechanical problems during a race. That clause has made racing a proving ground to benefit all mountain bikers by forcing designers, like myself, to create durable components. If road racing officials had maintained a similar self-sufficiency clause for the past seventy-five years, today's road bike would be significantly better.

To reduce bicycle racing, road or mountain, to a purely athletic endeavor is to ignore the broader benefits of race-driven technological advancements. The merger of human and machine is the most efficient form of personal transport. Bicycling transcends sport; it is healthy recreation and transportation. The bicycle is one of the most soulful, appropriate, and democratic inventions humans have ever devised. It keeps us connected to our surroundings as we travel under our own power.

For most of the twentieth century, bicycles remained relatively unchanged, more for reasons of being a backwater technology than having reached a state of perfection. But the immense popularity of the mountain bike, as well as its social implications, has attracted some of the world's most technically gifted minds to the industry, spurring development and advancing bicycles in general. The future may hold bicycles that are radically advanced from those ridden today.

Interestingly, the latter part of the nineteenth century saw the bicycle blossom during a similar burst of development. Bicycles accounted for two-thirds of U.S.

Patent Office volume between 1880 and 1900. Some of the sharpest minds of the day—James K. Starley, Col. Albert A. Pope, Albert Overman, and Thomas B. Jeffrey, to name a few—were in a mad race to advance the bicycle. Along the way the thriving industry perfected many of the building blocks of modern machinery and transport such as the pneumatic tire, ball bearing, roller chain, tensioned wire wheel and differential gearing. In addition the bicycle served as a stepping-stone for many engineers who later went on to shape the next incarnations of transportation—the automobile and the airplane. Among them were Henry Ford, Karl Benz, and the Wright brothers.

Automobiles and airplanes have of course increased our speed and mobility, but they haven't answered our need for exercise or a clean environment. Such shortcomings, which become more obvious as time passes, intensify our love and appreciation for the bicycle today.

Probably no aspect of mountain biking has pushed bicycle development more than downhilling, but it has also stirred the most controversy. The sport's "gonzo" image, associated with mountain biking from the beginning, has both promoted and impeded growth. During the 1980s the sport had been weaning itself from downhill competition because of increased trail-user conflicts. In 1990 however, some European countries insisted it be reinstated as the main event in world-class competition along with cross-country racing.

The renewed status of downhill racing and summer access to alpine ski-resort lifts have led to a resurgence in recreational downhilling popularity. Full-suspension downhill-specific bikes are the outcome. While I think it's the ultimate irony that driving to resorts and riding lifts renders the bike just another way to burn fossil fuels, interest generated from such activity will surely lead to more benign uses of bicycles, such as for everyday errands. Media coverage of the thrills and spills of downhill competition, while tending to reinforce the perception of bicycles as toys (just as auto racing glorifies cars as toys), is nevertheless exposure for bikes. When people try bikes and feel the benefits of exercise, it's only a small step to realizing a bike is great for many day-to-day uses and can actually save time.

Mountain bike trail access has long been an area of contention with other user groups. It's interesting that for many of the same reasons mountain biking became popular in Marin, it's being fought. There is a desire to enjoy our land and to protect it. The bottom line is that all mountain bikers need to ride responsibly and respect other users. Outdoor enthusiasts and clubs would all benefit by working together. Most environmentalists understand the benefits of using bikes for transportation, but many may not yet perceive mountain biking as a way to promote that use. Yet, mountain bikes are doing just that.

Riding a bike, at least riding responsibly, has always seemed to me a noble gesture. It promotes a vehicle that is good for the planet. It's a celebration of things sane. As someone who has helped the fat tire bike evolve from fifty-pound clunker to twenty-pound thoroughbred, my greatest satisfaction remains my role in helping inspire others to travel on two wheels under their own power. Our innocent tinkering with the mountain bike resulted in an infusion of vitality into cycling in developed countries worldwide.

Although bikes have been with us for more than 150 years, I truly believe the age of bicycling has only just begun. Who knows where bicycling will go from here. Anyone reading this book stands a fair chance of becoming a bicycling pioneer. Maybe someday *you* might say, "Heck, I was just havin' fun. . . ."

Joe Breeze, March 1998

History

Before the advent of pavement around 1890, all bikes were ridden off-road, so the fat tire bike we know today has a long lineage.

Mt. Tam's Mongrel

Since all bikes were ridden off-road before the advent of pavement around 1890, the fat tire bike we know today has a long lineage as well as a legacy of adventure and exploration. As evidence of this, one could look to the Klondike gold fields in the 1890s, where miners rode up the frozen Yukon River; to the Italian infantrymen during World War I, who shouldered bikes through the Alps; to the English inventor Vernon Blake, who promoted his "Bad Roads Bike" in the 1930s; or to the legendary father and son team of Ignaz and Frank W. Schwinn, who unveiled their balloon tire paperboy models to American kids in the mid-1930s.

An Iowa farm boy at mid-century probably didn't have to muster too much imagination to remove the fenders, chain guard, and bell from a Schwinn Excelsior so that he'd have a rattle-free, stripped-down rig to bomb over country roads toward his favorite swimming or fishing hole. And a few decades later it didn't require a great leap of engineering savvy to admire the advances in road riding technology (multiple gears, cantilever brakes, lightweight wheelsets) and wonder about applying them to the classic paper-boy ballooner. Long after ballooners had been marketed so successfully in the thirties and forties, isolated hobbyists—bike-shop mechanics, high school and college students, surfers—had been riding and retrofitting Schwinn bikes. They were cheap (nobody wanted them), heavy-duty (by virtue of their mass), and most of all, a gas to ride. These bikes went by a variety of names: ballooners, beaters, bombers, clunkers, cruisers, fat tire bikes.

It wasn't until the mid-1970s, however, amid the hills of 2,600-foot Mt. Tamalpais (a.k.a. Mt. Tam) in Marin County, just north of San Francisco, that a

Bob Burrowes

Gary Fisher

Kent Bostick

Donna Degan

Art Black

Mark Green

Joe Breeze

"THE ABILITY TO ASSEMBLE
ONE OF THESE BIKES WAS A
POWERFUL PIECE OF
KNOWLEDGE."

Gary Fisher

Michael Ducks

Alan Bonds

Les Degan

George Newman

Fred Wolf

Gordon Burns

Otis Guy

Chris McManus

Charlie Kelly

"CLUNKING OFFERED AN OUTLET FOR MY PRIMITIVE SIDE THAT I COULDN'T GET FROM ROAD RACING."

Joe Breeze

group of young cycling enthusiasts and budding entrepreneurs would dedicate themselves to improving the clunker concept, initiating a technological and marketing revolution that would completely redirect the bicycle industry. Northern California, a hotbed for road racing and outdoor activities, enjoyed an intellectual and business climate very open to innovation. Within a few short years these Marin County aficionados would create a bike complete with custom frame, thumb shifters, fifteen-speed derailleurs, and cantilever brakes. From just a few scavenged clunkers custom-assembled in the early 1970s, their innovations would account for nearly 85 percent of the 15.5 million new bike sales in 1996. And what started as casual races would spawn world championship events and, by the 1996 Centennial Games in Atlanta, reach full Olympic status.

Winds of change were blowing across Northern California in 1974. The Vietnam War was finally coming to a close. President Richard Nixon resigned, shaking America's faith in its power structure. Cars queued up at service stations to pay inflated prices for gasoline. Rock and roll anthems beckoned the younger generation to turn on, give peace a chance, and take charge of its future. The mainstream U.S. bicycle industry, with limited designs that were losing appeal among young riders, was coasting into a slump. All this was happening when the fat tire bike revolution began to take root in the Marin County towns of Fairfax, San Anselmo, and Mill Valley. The inhabitants living around Mt. Tam State Park and the Marin Municipal Water District open space were outdoor-oriented, and many had grown up hiking its miles of singletrack foot trails and fire roads.

The Pearl Pass Tour, originating in 1976, followed a rugged track built in Colorado in 1882 to haul gold and silver ore over the mountains between Crested Butte and Aspen. Pearl Pass rides were very influential in the early years of the modern fat tire bike's development.

A group of friends from the town of Larkspur began riding cast-off one-speed, coaster-brake, newsboy bikes on the dirt trails of Mt. Tamalpais as early as 1970. The heavy bikes were driven or walked to the top of the mountain, then the riders bombed down the steep trails, coaster brakes smoking. Once a year, these self-proclaimed Larkspur Canyon Gang riders ran a race from the top of the mountain back to Larkspur Canyon. Racers could choose any trail. According to one account, first prize was an envelope of marijuana, although the riders were not necessarily all pot smokers.

Charlie Kelly, in a 1979 *Outside Magazine* article, described some of their exploits:

> The canyon gangers were doing such stunts as riding at 40 miles per hour under a gate (with two inches of clearance above the handlebars) to maintain enough speed to launch the bike off a sharp crest for a 40-foot jump.

The fun-loving Canyon Gang soon disbanded, but one member, Marc Vendetti, joined Marin's road racing team, Velo Club Tamalpais, and introduced clunking to avid young road racing peers like Joe Breeze, Otis Guy, Gary Fisher, and Charlie Kelly. Riding these fifty-pound, one-speed, retro bikes appealed to these riders in a variety of ways, a number of whom, like Breeze and Fisher, were clocking between two hundred and five hundred miles per week on skinny-tired racers and vying in state and national events. Lumbering up Mt. Tam's switchbacks on these bikes in blue jeans and hiking boots also provided a novel and valuable training regimen.

"THE BIKE WAS A MOBILE PARTY. A WAY TO GET AWAY FROM THE COPS, THE CARS AND THE CONCRETE. WE WERE GOING PLACES WHERE THERE WASN'T ANYONE ELSE."

Gary Fisher

Above left: Campfire on the Pearl Pass route outside Crested Butte, Colorado, 1978. Above right: Action from "the Enduro," an early cross-country race, 1977. Center right (above): Charlie Kelly crossing the Little Kern River near Farewell Gap, now part of Sequoia National Park, 1978. Center right (below): Inspired rider at Pearl Pass, 1980. Center left: Joe Breeze, Vince Carlton, Fred Wolf, Gary Fisher, Charlie Kelly, and Eric Fletcher atop Marin's Mt. Barnaby for the sunrise. Lower right: Taking in the view on the north side of Mt. Tam.

"Clunking offered an outlet for my primitive side that I couldn't get from road racing," remembers Joe Breeze. "It wasn't long before many of us were experiencing ballooner mania." At the time, Breeze was fascinated by vintage bikes of all kinds, particularly turn-of-the-century models, which once represented the pinnacle in technology. "There was a wave of nostalgia sweeping through young people, but there was also a great interest in the potential of bicycles as a source of nonpollutive transportation."

Mt. Tamalpais was the proverbial mountain in the term *mountain bike*. Components were sought out that could withstand steep, winding descents, such as mid-century Morrow coaster brakes, long Ashtabula cranks, and Schwinn cantilever brakes. Cranksets had to be high enough so pedals wouldn't jam on rocks. These early bikes were mongrels, comprised of parts scavenged from classic cruisers and tandems, BMX bikes, and even motorcycles. Among the most influential of the early tinkerers was Gary Fisher, a Velo Club Tamalpais road racer and bike mechanic whose early custom clunkers spurred a flurry of innovation. Sometime after the December 1974 West Coast Open Cyclocross race in Marin—where Bernie and Russ Mahon, of Cupertino's Morrow Dirt Club, rode multiple-geared clunkers—Fisher built a Schwinn frame with multiple speeds, thumb shifters, and drum brakes that could ascend Mt. Tam's vertical grades. The Marin clunker riders were a social yet competitive bunch. Inspired by Fisher's improvements, it wasn't long before others in these off-road cliques outfitted their bikes similarly.

Other Marin County residents began to take notice. "The ability to assemble one of these bikes was a powerful piece of knowledge in those days. It was new territory," Gary Fisher recalls. "Turning people on to the sport was incredible because we were going places where there wasn't anyone else. The usual initial reaction was, 'What a hunk of junk!' Until they rode one, that is. Then their eyes would light up, as if you'd given them a marvelous drug."

Marin County riders prized one particular type of bicycle frame for clunking, the 1930s to 1940s Schwinn Excelsior. Its slack geometry and high bottom bracket, specified by a Schwinn engineer at a Chicago drafting table in the 1930s, held up moderately well to the rigors of Mt. Tam's descents; but sooner or later most frames cracked or snapped apart and had to be rewelded. The need for a better bike frame became obvious when the first Repack Downhill Race was held on Pine Mountain, just north of Mt. Tam, in 1976. The race got its name from the need to repack hub bearings after the grease sizzled out during the hair-raising four-and-a-half-minute descent. Alan Bonds, an early mountain bike pioneer, won that watershed first event. He was the only one who didn't fall or experience an equipment failure. Rider Wende Cragg recalls the race was terrifying. "I could never sleep the night before. Throughout the many years of the race, there was at least one broken collarbone and one guy almost scraped his nose off."

Joe Breeze remembers differently. "It was surprising how few people got hurt during those early years, basically because we were extremely good bike handlers—acrobats on wheels." The twenty-four ensuing Repack races would become essential to the development of fat tire bikes, generating enormous

Pete Barrett's poster for the first Repack Race—the competitive expression for the sport's early practitioners. Repack races offered the chance for competitors to assess the state of the art.

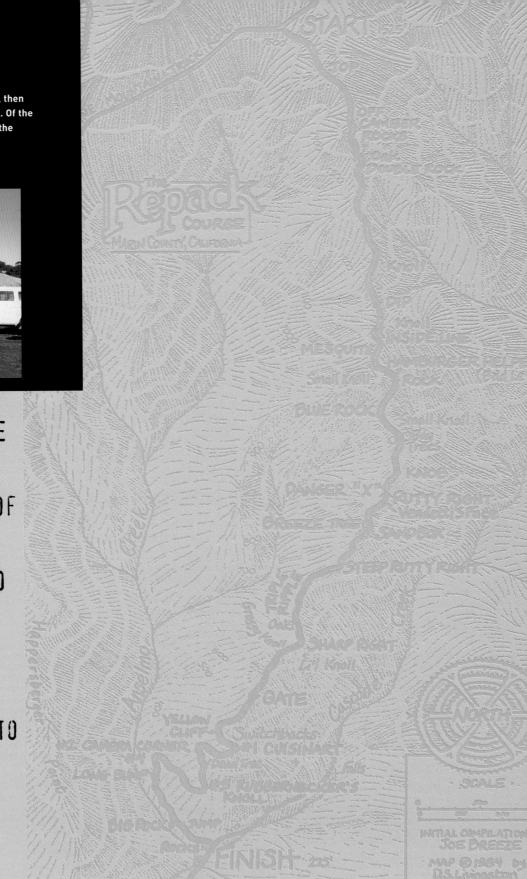

Riders hitched a ride to the top of Pine Mountain, then tested their technical skills with brakes smoking. Of the twenty-four Repack races held, Gary Fisher had the fastest time, Joe Breeze the most wins.

THEY CALLED THE RACE REPACK.

WITHIN FIVE MINUTES OF RIDING THE BRAKE ON PINE MOUNTAIN'S 1200 FOOT DESCENT, THE GREASE IN THE REAR HUB VAPORIZED.

THE HUB GREASE HAD TO BE REPACKED AFTER EVERY RUN.

Arnold, Schwinn & Co.

Introduces
Super
Balloon Tire
Bicycles

LOW PRESSURE
18 to 22 Lbs.
According to weight of rider

The only major development since the coaster brake—on the finest specially constructed bicycles built by the oldest and most outstanding American manufacturer. A 2⅛" automobile type double-tube, straight-side, cord tire—on a new deep drop center rim—a construction embodying all the latest advancements in the tire art.

ARNOLD, SCHWINN & CO.
1718 NORTH KILDARE AVE.
CHICAGO, ILLINOIS
TELEPHONE BELMONT 6793

Determined to steer the American bicycle industry out of a slump in the 1930s, Frank W. Schwinn introduced a line of balloon tire bikes that were a blast to ride and just looked fun. Schwinn had discovered the balloon tires on a trip to Europe. The bikes were an instant success and set the course for the company's dominance of the U.S. bike industry through the 1970s. Ironically, when the ballooner craze hit Marin four decades later, Schwinn's management failed to acknowledge that their innovation had come around full circle.

excitement and camaraderie around the new sport, and providing a venue for budding designers to share and assess each other's innovations. "Everyone was looking for a secret weapon," remembers Charlie Kelly.

When Joe Breeze designed his first hand-built fat tire bike frame in 1977, he adapted the form-flowing curvy geometry of the Schwinn Excelsior into a modernized straight-tube design. The Schwinn had a 70° head tube and a 70° seat tube; the modified Breezer featured a 68° head tube and a 70° seat tube. Instead of having the local paperboy in mind, as Ignaz and Frank W. Schwinn had, Breeze's models were himself and the six-foot, 180-pound Charlie Kelly. (Craig Mitchell had already made an experimental frame for Kelly, but it was more climber than downhill racer.) Breeze, a perfectionist, took months to produce his prototype from chrome moly tubing (specially strengthened steel). During the next half-year, he finished nine more nickel-plated thirty-eight-pound Breezers that sold for $750 each and included a tool kit. (Charlie Kelly's Breezer #2 now occupies a pedestal in the Mountain Bike Hall of Fame in Colorado, and Breeze's own #1 is in the Oakland Museum.) The most important aspect of Breeze's accomplishment was that he had advanced a cottage industry from one of assembly and retrofitting to full-scale custom production. Soon after producing what can be called the first modern mountain bike line, he took a leave of absence to attempt a cross-country tandem record with fellow road racer and fat tire enthusiast, Otis Guy.

In 1979, Gary Fisher and Charlie Kelly formed a company called MountainBikes. According to writer Frank Berto, the term *mountain bike* was originally coined by a clunker rider in Santa Barbara named Wing Bamboo. Fisher and Kelly were later unsuccessful in their bid to trademark the now generic name for the bike. For their source of frames, Fisher and Kelly turned to Tom Ritchey, a twenty-one-year-old whiz-kid racer who had established a reputation as a quality builder even before graduation from high school. Combining his

Joe Breeze brazing together one of his first ten Breezers. He was a meticulous craftsman with prior road frame building experience and was active in the off-road scene.

Breeze adapted the ergonomic geometry of the Schwinn Excelsior, but instead of heavy, curved, mild steel tubes, he used light, straight, chrome-moly steel tubes.

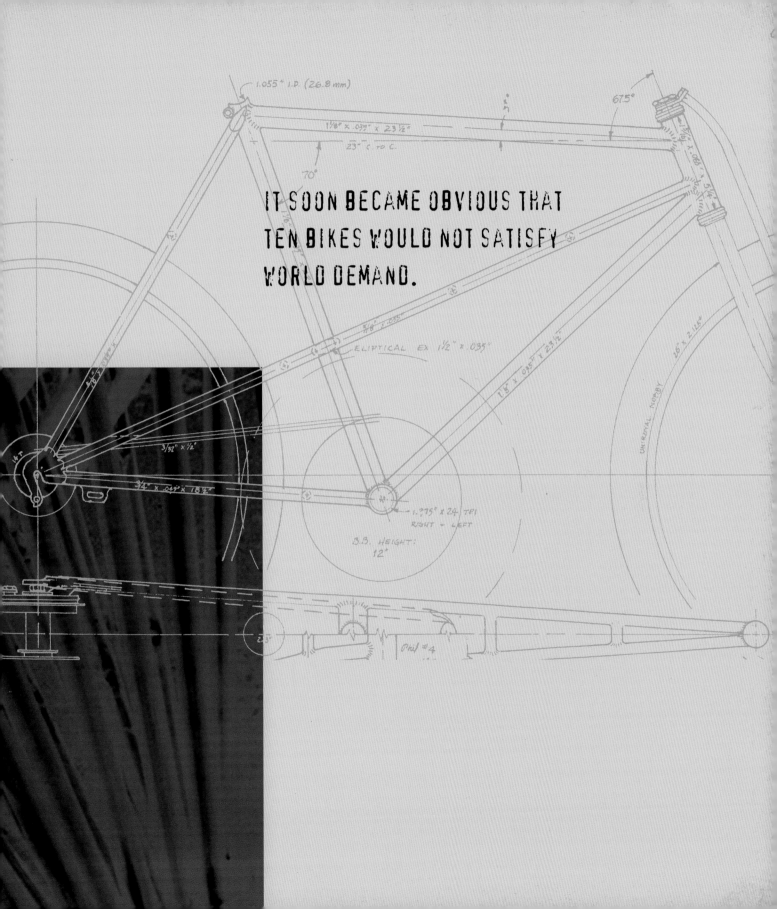

IT SOON BECAME OBVIOUS THAT
TEN BIKES WOULD NOT SATISFY
WORLD DEMAND.

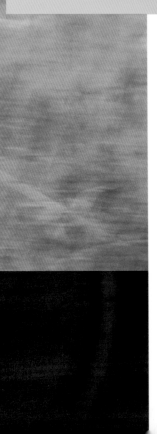

Above: Fred Wolf's Clunker, assembled on an old Schwinn frame by Gary Fisher in about 1975. Left: Fisher, at Tamarancho Boy Scout Camp in 1980. A top category racer, Fisher rode one of his early MountainBikes to victory at the 1980 Reseda-to-the-Sea race, establishing the viability of fat tire bikes as cross-country performers.

expertise with Breeze's important work, Ritchey provided high-quality frames that he could complete at an impressive speed. Fisher and Kelly assembled, marketed, and distributed the bikes to a growing base of up-scale customers willing to pay up to $1,500 for a bike they might wait four months to receive.

Japanese manufacturers Araya and Ukai had introduced twenty-six-inch aluminum rims for the adult BMX market by 1979, and in combination with 1980 CyclePro Snake Belly skin-wall mountain bike tires, the updated wheelsets shed an astounding six pounds off the bike weight. A 1980 MountainBike weighed only twenty-eight pounds.

The 150 MountainBikes that Fisher and Kelly sold in 1980 represented about half of the U.S. market. By this time, dozens of smaller builders around the country, including Mert Lawwill, Jeff Richman, Jeff Lindsay, Victor Vincente, Charlie Cunningham, and Erik Koski, were offering their own models and adding their own innovations. Among these smaller builders, Charlie Cunningham was altering the widely accepted Schwinn Excelsior frame geometry, and experimenting with new materials such as oversized aluminum tubing and magnesium handlebar stems, seat posts, and toe clips.

"In terms of innovations," says Cunningham, "everybody was standing on other people's shoulders. Everybody was learning from each other. And when the mountain bike craze happened, it had a life of its own. Suddenly there was more demand than supply, and the most important thing driving that demand was that mountain biking was fun."

Japanese manufacturers were carefully researching the Northern California designers with an eye to business opportunity. While large American and European manufacturers had dismissed the fat tire bike as a radical fringe, the Japanese had flexible manufacturing capabilities, an openness for new markets, and a very favorable exchange rate. "They drove up to our shops in Mercedes Benzes and popped out wearing suits and ties and brandishing cameras. Then they would punch out very cheesy versions of our stuff," remembers Cunningham, who at the time was flattered by the recognition. There is no question that eager suppliers capitalized on the young Marin builders, who often shared their unpatented ideas willingly in the interest of advancing their new sport.

At the 1982 Long Beach Bicycle Show, the industry's annual trade event, Specialized Bicycles, a San Jose–based company, introduced the Stumpjumper. In fact, the Japanese-made Stumpjumper was a near-exact replica of a MountainBike that Specialized founder Mike Sinyard had purchased the year before. At $750, the knock-offs were the hit of the show, and sold five hundred in just two weeks. "Even the color was the same," remembers Gary Fisher, who realized the Marin group had been out-maneuvered. (Ironically, it is a 1989 Stumpjumper, and not Fisher's Clunker or Breeze's Breezer, that now resides in the Smithsonian Institution's National Museum of American History.) Some weeks later, Univega, another California company, introduced the Alpina Pro, also Japanese-made. By year's end, dozens of manufacturers had jumped into the market, spurred on by overseas production and specially tailored component groups by Sun Tour and Shimano. Just one year after the Long

Charlie Cunningham, a founder of Wilderness Trail Bikes, a Marin company responsible for a number of developments, such as lightweight mountain bike tires and the first high-power brake.

A group of Japanese suppliers delights in Charlie Cunningham's first aluminum mountain bike frame, which even twenty years later impresses bike aficionados with its creative foresight. By 1982, Japanese production would make fat tire bikes more affordable to thousands of willing riders.

Beach trade show, there were two hundred thousand fat tire bikes on, and off, roads across America—up from ten Breezers in 1978.

Specialized C.E.O. Sinyard did more, however, than usher the Marin County invention into the age of global sourcing. He also launched an ad campaign that popularized the fun-loving lifestyle aspects of the bike. "It's not just a bike. It's a whole new sport," read the tagline on what would become years of successful ad campaigns. Even Fisher, who still bristles at the intellectual rip-offs that occurred during the early years, acknowledges that Specialized's marketing efforts helped to blow the market wide open. "You gotta surf the wave," he says, with a boyish twinkle in his eyes.

Breeze, Fisher, Kelly, Ritchey, Cunningham and many other pioneers not mentioned here had solved early technological hurdles. The bicycle was more user-friendly than ever before, and that design dynamic is still being improved upon today, as frame and component makers vie to produce lighter, stronger elements—and to introduce them sooner and more cheaply than anyone else. By the late 1980s, Gary Fisher would lay a claim to being the sole "inventor" of the mountain bike, a position he recanted a decade later. The sport had no single inventor, but evolved through a long series of individual technological contributions, some of which even went unremunerated and unrecognized. For many of the Marin pioneers, however, what was once known locally as "the world's tiniest sport" offered not only a quality lifestyle but a livelihood as well.

By 1983, MountainBikes was in financial straits, and Gary Fisher bought out partner Charlie Kelly; he later settled with frame supplier Tom Ritchey in a hostile split. Kelly continued as editor of the *Fat Tire Flyer*, the sport's only magazine, until 1985. Fisher and Ritchey formed their own companies. Trek ultimately bought Fisher's name and brought his design and marketing expertise under their corporate umbrella. This is just one example of how the sport's phenomenal success led to many founders' and innovators' companies being acquired by larger corporate entities.

With the proliferation of affordable bikes, the golden age of unlimited access to Mt. Tam's single tracks also soon came to a confrontational end. Hikers and equestrians became increasingly resentful of the ever-growing numbers of cyclists encroaching on their coveted territory, and the resulting rage boiled over into communities and wilderness areas in many regions of the country. In response to disputes over whether bikers should be permitted on trails previously used only as hiking trails and equestrian paths, concerned mountain biking associations, such as the National Off-Road Bicycling Association in 1983 and the International Mountain Biking Association in 1988, developed on-trail etiquette guidelines.

After just a dozen years, the public perception of a bicycle no longer included skinny tires, dropped handlebars, and hard-to-reach gear shifts on the down tube. By adapting the clunker into an easy-riding vehicle that performed in the back country, the fun-loving Marinites and others had tapped into a phenomenon that was much larger than most of them could have ever dreamed of. "The mountain bike was a secret, that once shared, changed people forever," Fisher wrote in 1997. "To watch it spread, bringing joy to the world, made my contemporaries and I feel like true contributors to society." No matter where people live today, they can somehow benefit from the movement, in terms of individual fitness, practical transportation, a sense of environmental responsibility, or just the exhilarating exhaustion that comes from pushing personal limits.

Technology

The fat tire bike is an industrial art form, an amalgam of diverse influences: motorcycles and aeronautics, metallurgy and sculpture, extreme sports and the triathlon.

The Anatomy of a Bike

The fat tire bike is an industrial art form, an amalgam of diverse influences: motorcycles and aeronautics, metallurgy and sculpture, extreme sports and the triathlon. There seems to be no limit to the speed or terrain mountain bikers reach for, and each successive plateau is achieved, in some part, by advances in technology. The examples presented in this chapter represent some of the most advanced technology the industry had to offer at the time of this writing. With time, evolving manufacturing capabilities should bring many of these design concepts within the financial reach of the average consumer.

Through the 1980s and 1990s, the sport benefited from the excess production capacity of the Japanese bike parts industry and affordable Taiwanese labor. The mountain bike's exploding market gave Japanese suppliers like Shimano and Sun Tour the opportunity to out-innovate and out-maneuver the European parts builders that had dominated the road bike market for so long. Talent wasn't hard to find on American shores, either. A slump in the West Coast aerospace industry left hundreds of engineers with time to ride bikes, and many began seeking work that could take advantage of their mastery of materials and machinery. Inventing bike components and concepts opened the doors to a new wave of entrepreneurship.

As the sport grew, more capital became available, and people discovered ways to make a living doing what they loved. Some small companies became empires as folks with big ideas for little toys got the chance to make their dreams real. Fat tire bikes became lighter, acquired more gears, and gained front and rear suspension.

The state of the art today is one of continued innovation, tempered by consolidation and commercialization. The spirit of the nutty professor or renegade builder that characterized the sport's early days has yielded to slick campaigns and sweeping technological changes designed to sell more and more products to a finite market. Yet off-roading remains one of the purest and most accessible expressions of advanced technology available to consumers. Few product categories remain so innovative—and so fun.

Technology, to a large degree, is what bikes are all about. And the anatomy of a mountain bike comprises a deceptively complex subject. This is partly because the science remains so hotly contested, but also because design and assembly entail such a wide range of decisions. From endless options about frame geometry and metals to variations in suspension and gearing, the combinations boggle the mind. Of course, there are no absolutes, only right designs, and the industry seems to be a magnet for inventors lured in by the age-old challenge: "It simply can't be done."

Frames

Ask ten mountain bike builders what frame materials they prefer, and you'll walk away with ten different opinions about the wide spectrum of materials available. To make things even more confusing, each material has endless variations that alter the ride and handling. To finely tune the ride of a frame, a frame builder must be part scientist and part alchemist.

Tom Ritchey has said that "a frame, when it is designed correctly, is probably as sophisticated as a B-1 bomber." For many riders, the traditional diamond design that has been the mainstay of steel frames since the early twentieth century is still the most elegant and efficient. Suspension technology, however, has created a split in the road, leaving two broad frame-design categories—"hardtail" (a diamond frame with a suspension fork) and "softtail" (the new full-suspension frame with shocks at both front and rear). Aluminum, titanium, and carbon fiber have greatly challenged traditional designs in recent years as well, and one can only be excited about what possibilities the future may hold as frame design unfolds.

Soul of the Machine

Steel

Steel is admittedly not the most cutting-edge stuff. It wasn't created by NASA for the lunar rover, and it doesn't end in *-ium*. But steel endures in a world of boutique alloys because it is inexpensive, durable, and practical; above all, it offers such an exceptional quality ride.

There was a time when steel had more romance. Reynolds, an English metal manufacturer supplying bicycle tubing as early as 1898, patented the very first high-tech frame material in 1935—double-butted steel tubing. (Double-butted tubing is thicker at the ends, where it is welded, and thinner in the middle, making it light and strong.) The company's 531 brand was the mark of a top-of-the-line frame for decades. In 1995, Reynolds introduced its first new tubing in over twenty years, the 853 tubeset, one of a new breed of superswteels. It's no stiffer than other steels, but undergoes a process called "air hardening" after welding that makes it stronger, so less can be used.

It's almost painful to pigeonhole steel for one purpose over another. For years, it's been the sport's absolute workhorse, but recent market trends have nearly reduced steel to a material used exclusively on low- to mid-priced hardtail off-road rigs. Steel has lost ground to aluminum and titanium in bikes that are considered to be truly off-road ready, and is all but absent on today's full-suspension rigs. One place where steel still has a dedicated following is among small custom-frame builders, who retain their love for the material and continue to craft light, beautiful bikes from the ferrous alloy.

Master of Steel

Before Tom Ritchey was old enough to vote, he built 250 bike frames. And in the twenty-odd years since that time, his shop has produced upwards of ten thousand. Perhaps no other frame builder in the world has been born with such innate focus and prolific talent. Grant Peterson, publisher of the *Rivendell Reader*, has written that "he's at a level—and he's been at that level since he was young—where his fellow frame builders don't seem to regard him as competition. Since frame builders are human, there is a certain amount of envy, but it's overshadowed by respect, admiration, and a hint of the type of reverence usually reserved for the dead."

Ritchey's mastery is predicated on a devotion to steel. He can transform a set of steel tubes into a frame before lunchtime (including paint) and even have time for coffee breaks. Yet he estimates that frame building takes up a mere ten percent of his time as C.E.O. of Ritchey Design in Redwood City, California. The rest of his days are spent designing tires and components, managing a team of qualified employees, and riding between eight and ten thousand miles per year. Once an exceptional junior racer himself, Ritchey also has a knack for picking racing talent before it blossoms. Team Ritchey riders have won more world championships and world cup races than any team on the off-road circuit.

Ritchey custom-butted steel hardtail frame with sloping seat stays. Few other designers have pushed the material to its limits of lightness and ductility.

Aluminum

The aluminum revolution began in Van Nuys, California, with Easton Sports, a company known for producing baseball bats that pinged, rather than oversized bike tubes; but it turned out that Easton's skill at replacing a traditional material with a high-tech substitute would eventually make aluminum the metal of choice for the vast majority of off-road bikes. Easton designer Chuck Teixiera collaborated with John Parker, of Yeti Cycles, a small, innovative frame shop then located in Los Angeles, to create an aluminum tubeset equal to the task.

"We wanted a frameset that was sophisticated," Teixiera recalls. "Something that outperformed aluminum's reputation for a harsh and unforgiving ride."

Aluminum bikes had been around for years, but the new ProGram tubeset Teixiera and Parker created significantly reduced manufacturing time. Easton also engineered a marketing coup. Since it was not a bike company, Easton made the tubesets available to any manufacturer who showed the ability to work with them. Within a few years, dozens of builders—from giants like Trek to tiny custom shops like Colorado's 3D Racing—were building and selling ProGram bikes.

John Parker and Yeti Cycles were extremely influential in advancing the use of aluminum tubing in high performance bikes. Many fat tire pros began their careers on alumium frame Yeti cycles.

Why have builders tried for decades to build frames from aluminum? As a low-density material, it provides thin-walled, oversized tubes economically that are great for full-suspension frames, where the only rule regarding tubing is the stiffer, the better. "Most riders equate aluminum with the lightness of a beer can," says Sky Yaeger, product manager for Bianchi U.S.A. "The weight factor alone seems to sell aluminum frames to bike buyers without regard to issues of durability or repairability."

Since the mid-1990s, an aluminum frame, made of cheaper Taiwanese tubing, and front suspension have rendered the low-end steel hardtail almost obsolete. Affordable dual-suspension aluminum bikes loom on the horizon.

Paolo Salvagione, founder of Swift Cycles.

Specialty Craftsman

"I like sitting in a cafe near the end of the day and looking at a bunch of my bikes covered with mud," says Paolo Salvagione, one of many custom bike builders making a living in Northern California. Salvagione set up his shop—Swift Cycles—along the Sausalito waterfront, where he produces one or two beautifully crafted frames a month, primarily from titanium and aluminum. He is also reputed in the industry for his good repair and design services, and he is a student and collector of bicycle history.

"One of the strengths of aluminum is its rigidity, which means the frame will flex very little when you're pushing down on the pedals and climbing," says Salvagione. Unfortunately, that can make for a harsh ride. "To offset that, I make a rather long, large-diameter, thin-walled seat post that flexes when ridden. This creates a sort of passive suspension. Overall the design creates a rigid bike that is great for climbing, yet comfortable for everyday riding."

Salvagione says that his greatest satisfaction comes from building things without internal combustion engines. "I don't get into the question of which material is better," he says. "I agree with Buckminster Fuller, who said there are no wrong materials, just wrong designs."

Titanium

Titanium is a relative newcomer to the bicycle world. Early mountain bike frames crafted from titanium date back to 1984, when Gary Helfrich began experimenting with the material in Boston. (Road frames of titanium had cropped up as early as the 1950s, most notably with the Teledyne Titan race bike of the 1970s.) In 1986, Mike Augspurger, Gary Helfrich, and Gwyn Jones founded Merlin Metalworks and introduced titanium bikes that were gorgeous and rode beautifully. (Litespeed Titanium Bicycles began selling titanium bikes around the same time.) Merlin crafted framesets from an alloy of 94.5 percent titanium, 3 percent aluminum, and 2.5 percent vanadium. Known as 3Al/2.5v titanium, this alloy is now the most common in all titanium bike frames from Merlin and its many competitors.

The most well-known characteristics of titanium are strength, resilience, and anti-corrosiveness; it has a ride quality that can be described as lively and comfortable. The material's biggest downside is cost, with titanium frames starting at least 25 percent higher than the finest custom-made aluminum and steel hardtails. The high price has led to the assumption that titanium is a rare metal, but it isn't; refining

The Ibis Bow-Ti uses titanium's flex characteristics to create five inches of travel with no pivots.

and extracting the metal is what costs so much. It is extremely difficult to build a good titanium frame, because the welding tolerances are so precise and have to be executed in an inert environment.

Titanium is primarily used to make light, hardtail mountain bike frames that can cost as much as motorcycles. Its use in full-suspension bikes is limited because aluminum works fairly well and costs much less. Litespeed Titanium Bicycles, a family-owned metal business in Ooltewah, Tennessee, has succeeded in producing relatively reasonably priced titanium frame bicycles, and popularizing the notion of recreational uses for this traditionally aeronautical material. Titanium, however, remains the realm of medium- and small-sized shops, such as One-Off Titanium Inc., Merlin Metalworks, Swift Cycles, Seven Cycles, Arctos Machine, Ibis Cycles, and others.

**Scot Nicol,
founder of Ibis Cycles.**

Revolutionary Detail

Ibis Cycles, of Sebastapol, California, has earned a reputation for lightweight, high-performance bikes and meticulous attention to detail. Founder Scot Nicol apprenticed with veterans Joe Breeze and Charlie Cunningham before establishing his company in 1981. "I chose the name by leafing through an Audubon bird guide," he says. "Naming a bike after a bird has been an industry tradition reaching way back."

Over the years, Ibis has not only become known for its no-compromise approach to quality, but for risk-taking as well. In 1996, the company slam-dunked the industry with the Bow-Ti, a revolutionary frame conceived by maverick engineer John Castellano that created a pivotless dual-suspension bike with five inches of travel. Other frames required pivots because of the rigidity of aluminum, but the Bow-Ti used the flex of titanium to eliminate the pivot, pushing the material to its full extreme.

"John Castellano is a wizard," Nicol says of his longtime friend and collaborator. "He thought up the Bow-Ti while riding up Railroad Grade on Mt. Tam one day, outmaneuvering dozens of engineering teams across the country who'd been trying to make a better titanium frame design."

Composites

In the 1990s, frame builders struggled to build durable frames with ultralight, super-strong composites like carbon fiber and thermoplastic. It was obvious that carbon fiber combined tremendous strength and stiffness with light weight. Since it can be four times lighter and stronger than steel, even the largest manufacturers grappled with the simple problem of how they could actually join carbon-fiber tubes. Welding isn't possible, so manufacturers tried bonding and mechanical joining methods. They tried gluing the tubes into lugs from aluminum or carbon fiber. When this proved ineffective, manufacturers turned to making monocoque (molded) carbon fiber frames that eliminated joints completely.

Trek's full-suspension Y-bike is among the most successful composite bikes ever made. It uses a monocoque main frame combined with an aluminum rear triangle. Cannondale's Raven full-suspension bike uses an aluminum skeleton wrapped in carbon fiber sheets, a development many believe could be the future of the material.

Cannondale, the company that put aluminum on the map, is now a leader in composite technology. The Raven features an aluminum spine wrapped with a carbon-fiber shell.

Suspension Forks and Shocks

The dominant type of forks are telescopic. The lower legs are suspended by a spring medium and slide over the fixed upper stanchions. Brands include RockShox, Answer Manitou, Marzocchi, or Cannondale HeadShok forks. A spring doesn't always mean a coiled piece of metal. Compressed air, elastomers (urethane bumpers), or a combination of these materials can provide the suspension action. Answer Manitou's 1998 flagship, the SX-Ti, is a good example of the telescopic fork. It uses both coil and elastomer springs and has an oil-filled damping cartridge to control the compression and return rate of the springs.

Linkage suspension—long popular on early balloon tire bikes and motorcycles—is now being popularized by Girvin, of Woonsocket, Rhode Island, and Mert Lawwill of Yeti Cycles in Durango, Colorado. Linkage forks use two sets of blades—one fixed to the fork crown and one attached to a spring medium—that are connected by a small, articulating link. When the wheel encounters any upward force, the link pushes the nonfixed set of fork blades up, compressing the shock.

Paul Turner, founder of RockShox

Shock Mogul

The mountain bike took a decidedly faster downhill course in 1987, when Paul Turner, a factory Honda motorcycle designer living in Santa Cruz, created the first prototype RockShox suspension mountain-bike fork. The initial prototype fork was developed by Turner and Santa Cruz frame-building legend Keith Bontrager. Suspension forks gave the mountain bike "travel," or the ability to cushion an impact with fast-reacting shock absorbers. Making a fork that could compress, then retract was an idea inventors had experimented with since the late nineteenth century.

By 1989, the first hundred RockShox RS-1 forks had rolled out of a small Boulder, Colorado, facility, and a boom in mountain-bike suspension was about to start. In 1996, RockShox shipped their millionth fork and made Paul Turner one of the industry's most successful entrepreneurs. "I have a greedy agenda," says Turner, "I want my bike to work better. Our future challenge is to develop a plush-riding, maintenance-free fork that weighs five pounds less."

The RockShox RS-1, the first mass-produced front suspension fork, redirected the fat tire industry.

The HeadShok super downhill fork features air-sprung, oil-dampened compression mechanisms.

Racing has been the driving force behind improving suspension. RockShox's 2.9-pound, SID (Superlight Integrated Design) was developed for top cross-country racers who wanted a fork that was super-light and could be adjusted to respond only to large bump forces.

The Boxxer, a downhill-specific component, is a lightweight version of a motocross fork. It weighs eight pounds and sells for a staggering price.

For Bob Fox, who had been designing and manufacturing suspension parts for motorcycles, cars, and snow-mobiles since 1975, the mountain bike market seemed an obvious outlet for his company's expertise. In 1991, Fox introduced one of the industry's first rear shocks, and he has since become a main supplier in the full-suspension bike segment. Fox, who produces both an air shock and a spring shock, believes evolution in design and engineering will continually improve full suspension's already cushy ride. All he was willing to give away is that "the changes will be more than cosmetic."

Suspended Innovation

Doug Bradbury

Doug Bradbury is one of the legendary innovators of the sport's modern era—meaning the era of aluminum and suspension. "I turned to mountain biking because I kept getting hurt on motorcycles, and Ferrari didn't need a new Formula One driver," says Bradbury. "But the bikes just didn't work well enough. I was on the ground all the time. I wanted to make a bike that handled correctly, so I didn't have to pick myself up all the time."

Unlike RockShox by Turner and Bontrager, who essentially shrunk a motorcycle fork, Bradbury's Manitou fork was packed in urethane. The big break came when John Parker of Yeti Cycles introduced him to John Tomac. The world-class racer rode the prototype Manitou fork to a national championship, and the inventor went from living in a garage to millionaire status within a couple of years. Today the company, called Answer Manitou, is RockShox's principal rival in the suspension fork business, and Bradbury's Colorado-based design shop sells a range of cutting-edge products.

Keith Bontrager

For Keith Bontrager, who says he was too small to play baseball, football, or basketball, mountain biking has always been a main source of physical and mental fitness. "I get stronger, braver, smarter, and more coordinated when I ride," he says.

The founder of Bontrager Cycles, he is a product designer who takes performance and safety criteria to levels most designers might consider extreme. Today, Bontrager does most of his riding on the singletracks winding through the redwood forests near Santa Cruz. "But I'm not a bliss ninny," he says. "I don't mind earning turns and working hard at it. Then, being the technically inclined sort that I am, there are the hardware challenges, how to make the things better. Riding and tinkering is most of what I think about and do, and I'm lucky enough to get paid for it."

Shimanopoly

Look at any mountain bike, and the chances are very good that the majority of its components will be stamped with the S-word. Though significant competitors exist—Grip Shift's gearing systems, Sugino's cranks, Avid's brakes—the Japanese giant Shimano asserts a Microsoft-like dominance, with over 90 percent of the off-road components market. There's a simple reason. Shimano has made drive trains that shift effortlessly, pedals that allow you to stomp and go at will, and V-brakes that have kept pace with the rapid speeds achieved on downhill racing rigs.

With a hundred engineers in Japan and a U.S. crash-test team dubbed Skunk Development (after Lockheed's fabled Skunk Works), Shimano has one of the industry's strongest and largest financial commitments to R & D and quality control. Originally founded in 1921 to supply single-speed freewheels for English-style bikes of the day, Shimano has pioneered sweeping innovations time and again, occasionally drowning its competitors in a sea of unsold inventory.

"By designing components with a systems approach as far back as the 1970s," says Shimano product manager Steve Boehmke, "we were able to make components that worked better together than what had traditionally been coming from Europe. The European approach at that time was that you could mix and match any components on your bike. We found that if you made a set of derailleurs to match the cogs that worked with the chain that was designed to go on certain chainrings, you could vastly improve the performance of the bicycle and its drivetrain."

Shozaburo Shimano (right) when Shimano Iron Works was founded in 1921.

Throughout the 1980s, the fat tire components market was equally divided between Shimano and its rival Sun Tour, whose systems were technically innovative and often more user-serviceable; but Shimano gearing always seemed to shift just a little better. By the early 1990s, the company had replaced the old, beloved, and elegantly simple thumb shifters with more complicated RapidFire setups. Though there were many protests, the truth was that RapidFire worked better. As Shimano refined the system, Sun Tour faded into the background. The company expanded its dominance by designing systems that were dependent on each other: cranks and bottom brackets; chains and freewheels; brakes and levers. Manufacturers found it inconvenient, if not difficult, to choose non-Shimano parts for their new bikes.

Companies that sought to outdo Shimano with computer-machined parts found out that the Japanese manufacturer's ability to unveil line after line of light, cold-forged accessories was insurmountable. Many are looking to Grip Shift—which acquired European component maker Sachs—as the next-best chance to rival Shimano. Given the way the Japanese giant has risen to every challenge in the past, vanquishing nearly all comers, it is probably an opportunity Shimano relishes as well.

RapidFire bar-end shifter.

RapidFire thumb and trigger system.

Drivetrain

The drivetrain encompasses the bike's engine and transmission: shifters, front and rear derailleurs, chain, cogs, crankset, and bottom bracket. (The fuel tank rests on the saddle.) Current mountain bikes generally have front and rear derailleurs that shift a chain onto any of twenty-four different gear combinations (three chainrings in front and up to nine cogs in the rear). Manufacturers and inventors continue to experiment with non-chain-based systems that would give the bike a transmission akin to that of a car or motorcycle, but weight, durability, and cost have been tough obstacles. The durable, efficient solution of the derailleur first introduced in 1912 still rules today.

Shifters

Shimano's RapidFire shifters use a trigger-like system, where the rider pushes or pulls either of two levers, one mounted on each side of the handlebar. Twist-type shifters—from Grip Shift and Sachs—work like a throttle: the rider rotates a small grip on either side of the handlebar to select the proper gear. In reality, both systems work quite well, with a functional difference akin to the "boxers versus briefs" debate.

Grip Shift twist-shifting system.

Derailleurs

The rear derailleur, which moves the chain up and down as many as nine rear cogs while maintaining chain tension, is probably the most intricate component on a bicycle. To road riders of the 1950s, 1960s, and 1970s, the classic Campagnolo derailleurs seemed to work as well as anyone thought possible. The mountain bike changed all that, however, challenging a European road-riding establishment that flaunted innovation and asserted that the superior athlete should win, not the one with the better hardware. The need to shift a mud-spattered chain under a heavier load and higher torque pushed the development of the derailleur fast and far. Japan's Sun Tour Slant Pantagraph, a mountain-ready rear derailleur and thumb-shifter combination, was preferred in the sport's early years, but by 1990, the Shimano Deore drivetrain had won the battle. It simply shifted better, greatly reducing the chance of gear jamming on steep uphill climbs, when reliable shifting is needed most.

Sram ESP rear derailleur.

Today, XTR—with its ultralight derailleur and shifter combo—is the racer's choice.

Functional and pricey, Cannondale's Coda series—
originally designed by Alex Pong—features crank
arms bonded from two oversized, clam-shell halves
that create a super-light and rigid result. The
Shimano XTR crankset is channel-forged, then
capped for stiffness and strength. Both work only
with proprietary bottom brackets.

Cranksets

Every technology comes full circle, and so it is with the crank, which propels the chain. In the early 1990s, small manufacturers launched an off-road fashion craze with garishly colored anodized cranks made of machined aluminum. Though the garage-built cranks were better looking and lighter than their Asian counterparts, they were also more expensive and, in most cases, qualitatively inferior to the forged competition. Today, most cranksets on new off-road bikes are of forged aluminum, made by large manufacturers such as Shimano and Sugino, who can afford the enormous start-up costs. Durability and functionality have won out over boutique flair.

Pedals

Advances in pedal technology have probably improved the experience of the average rider more than anything, including suspension. Like ski bindings, clipless pedals essentially render the rider "one with the bike," increasing efficiency, control, and safety—after a few rides are spent getting used to them. Among the first to modernize the concept in the early 1980s was Boone Lennon, chief engineer for Scott U.S.A. His clipless design used a protruding cleat that fit into a metal slot in the top of a typical platform pedal. Only a few prototypes were made. The Shimano SPD system set the standard for most modern competitors because it was durable and let riders get off their bikes and clamber over rocks and stumps without killing themselves—or walk down the aisle of the local market without sounding like Fred Astaire.

Step-in pedals, like ski bindings, are available with a wide range of platforms and cleat systems. Among the design factors are float, which allows the cleats to move, easing stress on the knees, and clearance, which can minimize the accumulation of mud and dirt.

Wheels

About wheels, Keith Bontrager comments, "Light, strong, or cheap. Pick two." Attempts to circumvent this rule of thumb have given rise to new types of wheels, among them one-piece composites that are said to be stronger. But the truth is that the basic hub, wire spoke, and metal rim design of the wheel, developed over a century ago by some of the sharpest minds of the day, hasn't changed much. If industry expansion catches up with recent engineering developments in composite technology, however, the wheel could indeed be in for a wave of reinvention.

Spinergy popularized the half carbon-fiber and half aluminum rim for the mountain bike.

Complete Wheels

Complete wheelsets—rim, hubs, and spokes—are now commonly built by one manufacturer, because when each part of a wheel is designed with the others in mind, the set can be harmonized and optimized for the greatest strength and lowest weight. In the summer of 1996, with the Olympic Games only a few weeks away, Mavic introduced the CrossMax and CrossLand wheelsets, which use fewer spokes (twenty-four as opposed to thirty-two in a traditional wheel) with much higher tension and a super-thin-walled, box-shaped, ceramic coated rim to shave weight while increasing durability. Other manufacturers quickly followed. There is a drawback to this approach, however. Complete wheels must be sent back to the manufacturer for rim replacement, potentially inconveniencing a rider for a couple weeks.

Composite Wheels

After many years of heavy investment and education, Spinergy is beginning to break down the stereotypes of expense and fragility that composite wheels have long faced. In fact, these wheels greatly minimize maintenance and maximize style. Composite wheels appeared in Olympic road and track heats in the early 1980s, and the first three-spoked, mountain-worthy versions were introduced by Tri-Spoke and Specialized in 1989. But it wasn't until 1993 that a Rutgers University graduate student named Raphael Schlanger reinvented the off-road wheel in thermoplastic under the Spinergy brand name. Connecticut-based Spinergy uses a patented technology to give pairs of carbon spokes—bonded to a carbon-fiber and aluminum rim—enough tension to support the entire wheel.

ABOUT WHEELS, KEITH BONTRAGER SAYS, "LIGHT, STRONG, OR CHEAP. PICK TWO."

DT Hugi front and rear hubs feature a unique ratcheting system and unparalleled durability.

The Paul Rear Single Speed Hub is made specifically for that emerging category of riding.

Hubs

The front hub has a simple job: to anchor the spokes and prevent the legs of a suspension fork from acting independently. Most quality front hubs now use sealed cartridge bearings and maximize the surface area of the hub that contacts the fork dropout (the slot where the wheel fits into the fork) to increase bending stiffness.

Rear hubs, which contain the freewheel mechanism (the source of the bicycle's unmistakable whir) are a monument to snazzy industrial design and complex engineering. The bulk of today's rear mountain-bike hubs use a free-hub mechanism that integrates the freewheel (cassette cog) directly into it. The advantage of this, because the hub's bearings are farther apart, is greater support for the rear axle.

Rims

Between 1980 and 1981, innovations shaved six pounds from rim and tire. In recent years, advanced technology such as Finite Element Analysis and ultra-precise extruding have taken lighter and more durable rims to entirely new plateaus. Experts largely concur that rims designed with a modified box cross-section form (where a cutout view of the rim looks like a box with its top flaps extended to hold the tire) yield the best strength-to-weight ratio.

  Two huge advances were recently introduced by French manufacturer Mavic, the world's largest producer of high-quality bicycle rims. The first is Mavic's "Souder Usine Process" (SUP for short) for joining a rim. Rims start as flat extrusions of aluminum that are rolled into a hoop and joined together in perfect alignment, eliminating an often troublesome seam that would cause the brake pads to make a thumping noise when applied. Rather than pinning the rim ends together mechanically, Mavic welds them, then precision grinds the braking surface of each rim to a mirror-flat finish. Mavic's other big gift to mountain bikers everywhere was the application of a ceramic powder coating that increases friction in wet or dry conditions and extends a rim's life through years of rigorous braking.

Mavic's newest generation of rims has improved stopping power in all weather conditions.

Choosing a mountain bike tire can be a difficult process as the number of terrain- and performance-specific tread designs continues to multiply. The emerging science of fat tire design has brought the sport a long way from the balloon tires of the early days. There are tires that fold and tires for sand, mud, dirt, slickrock and asphalt. Soon, we are told, there will be tires that never flat.

Tires and Treads

For years, the big tire trend has been to design tires with very specific, narrow uses. Tire manufacturers offer cross-country tires specially designed for an incredible variety of precise soil conditions: hard, sandy, loamy, sloppy mud, and even just for use on the famous Slickrock trail outside of Moab, Utah. Following in the steps of the European firm Corratec, who produced the semi-slick for its pro racing team in 1995, every major tire manufacturer currently offers a similar design for high-performance riding and cross-country racing. Semi-slick tires have a nearly bald center section and knobs along the edges, a combination that decreases rolling resistance in a straight line while maintaining cornering traction. Semi-slicks can be a handful on the downhills, but their fast ride on flat surfaces and climbs makes them a big favorite with the race crowd.

During the 1996 racing season, rumors began to circulate that Michelin was close to realizing the holy grail of bicycle tires: one that didn't go flat. *Le systeme* apparently uses a standard Michelin downhill tire and inner tube combined with some type of foam. Although Michelin's French World Cup race support crew is tight-lipped about its venture, it revealed that each tire takes more than an hour to prepare. Flat-proof tires could come to the masses by the turn of the century.

Yet another cross-pollination from the motorcycle world is the drum brake, which is just on the horizon. If the wheel rim is damaged on a ride, the stopping ability of drum brakes won't be affected.

Brakes

Brakes perform a basic function: quenching the increasing speeds that current innovation makes possible. Traditional cantilever brakes, which consist of two separate calipers mounted to the frame and the fork and tied together with a straddle cable, were favored for nearly a century; but by the mid-1990s, faster and faster bikes overwhelmed their capabilities.

Shimano's V-brake is a new type of highly powerful cantilever. The V-brake revolutionized the way bikes stop by using longer, vertically opposed brake arms to increase the unit's leverage and power. The finer points of Shimano's system were new, but the idea of using long-armed, vertically opposed cantilevers was initially modernized by Ben Capron, of Santa Cruz, who himself was evolving an existing concept. Capron's Marinovative brakes of the early 1990s used long pieces of aluminum trim for the cantilever arms, and are clearly the progenitor for today's benchmark stoppers.

Steve Potts

Shimano XTR-brakes have eclipsed the old cantilever system and set new standards for stopping power.

Disc brakes, like cantilevers, have been around in one form or another since the end of the nineteenth century. The most obvious feature of a disc brake is that it relies on a hub-mounted rotor, rather than the wheel rim, for a stopping surface. (Rims are sometimes damaged on a ride and go out of true, which can dramatically diminish brake performance.) Though weight and cost pose significant hurdles, it seems all but inevitable that disc brakes will someday become standard off-road equipment.

Wilderness Trail Bikes

Name the products that turned off-roading from a weekend hobby into a high-performance sport, and you'll likely have to give credit to Marin County's Wilderness Trail Bikes (WTB). Their innovations include lightweight, folding tires (that can easily be packed away), and the first super-stopping designer brakes. WTB spent much of the 1980s and 1990s acting as a shadow design shop for dozens of the sports biggest names, including Specialized, Sun Tour, Blackburn, and Araya.

WTB's four partners—Charlie Cunningham, Steve Potts, Mark Slate, and Patrick Seidler—each bring a sense of individual passion to WTB's very unstructured structure. Cunningham is an off-road original, a classic workshop tinkerer who best fits WTB's mad-scientist role. Potts is a master framebuilder and the company's genial face. He can often be found riding Mt. Tam with his son on a custom-built child seat. Slate is also a master designer, and Patrick Seidler is the company's designated "suit."

WTB has begun marketing more products under its own brand name, including tires, wheelsets, and framesets. Cunningham, especially, has stood in opposition to the trend of disposable bike parts that the average consumer can't maintain. This often makes WTB gear more expensive than most, but the company's diehard fans seem willing to pay the price. The company is heavily involved in bike advocacy, and was closely associated with the New Paradigm trail, a legendary protest singletrack built surreptitiously on Mt. Tam—and destroyed after its discovery.

Saddles

There's a seat for every bottom: seats with holes in the middle, seats with the sides cut off, seats with a power ridge on the back, seats with the nose curved radically downward. Seats with gel, air, or water padding. Seats with sheepskin covers and separate pads for each buttock, seats that look like doughnuts, and, of course, seats that look like sparkly bananas. Bread-loaf-sized downhill seats from such manufacturers as Tioga, SDG, and Scott, used not so much for comfort as for control, are the latest trend. With the ability to slide forward and back, the downhill rider can better distribute weight on the bike.

Stems

The stem positions and holds the handlebars in place, and aluminum has become the choice material for the same reasons it is the most popular in frame and handlebar markets: it is cheap, light, and easy to work with. Titanium is a fantastic material for stems, but whether you're making frames, handlebars, stems, or anything else from the grayish metal, it's still incredibly expensive. Steel, the dominant stem material in the 1980s and still the favorite of many, has steadily lost market share to both lighter, less expensive stems made of aluminum and sexy boutique titanium models.

Innovative stem designs, such as these by the Canadian manufacturer Syncros, are efficient and mechanically advanced and make changing handlebars easier than ever before.

Headsets

The King headset has an Olympian reputation in the fat tire industry for its amazing durability and functionality.

The headset is the main set of bearings on which the fork rotates. Headsets don't have to do much, but good ones must stay smooth and free of play in even the muddiest of conditions. Chris King—an avid cyclist and machinist from Santa Barbara—introduced the first high-quality cartridge-bearing headset in 1976, years before mountain bikes became popular. King's headsets featured precision machining for unmatched smoothness, a stainless steel bottom race for superior longevity, and sealed cartridge bearings for years of trouble-free service. King headsets have changed little over the years, a tribute to the perfection and foresight of his decades-old design.

Handlebars

Handlebar styles change as fast as hem lines in Paris. The first production mountain bikes, such as the early Specialized Stumpjumpers, used aluminum handlebars with sharply upswept middle sections and flat ends. Then, for nearly a decade, flat bars with no rise or drop and only a slight three- or five-degree back sweep dominated the market. However, with the increase in popularity of downhill racing and freeriding (two disciplines where riders seek a more centered, upright position) a refined and redesigned version of early rise bars has gained popularity.

This rigidity-enhancing cross brace is yet another example of a motorcycle component adapted for the bicycle.

Though most bars are made from aluminum, other materials are also employed. One option is carbon fiber, as in this one from L.P. Composites Inc.

Garb

Accessories seem to become increasingly compact, lightweight, convenient, and more expensive all the time. Energy bars, water carriers, and tube foods keep you from bonking; tool kits, high pressure pumps, and patches help maintain inflation; shoes, socks, gloves, and shades are indispensible basics. You can revel in the variety of coordinating and clashing colors and decide for yourself which are relevant.

1997

1975

1983

1986

1992

1994

1995

Helmets

Helmets go by a number of names: brain bucket, skid lid, and brain sieve, to name a few. Protecting your bean in comfort and style has been a dynamic process. Lightweight foam products developed in the early years have given way to newer assembly methods which effectively combine both plastic and foam. Shapes have become more aerodynamic. Vents have made helmets lighter and more comfortable. And safety standards have continually increased. Two important innovations in the series at right were the rear Roc Loc, which limits wobble, and the visor, which deflects the elements. (Both are on the helmet, second from the bottom.)

Culture

Mountain biking is an integral part of our modern identities, transcending generations, income levels, geographic boundaries, and physical capabilities. It is a vehicle for competition, commerce, artistic expression, fashion, friendly association, and pilgrimage.

Medalists, Messengers, and Mavericks

Fat tire culture has quickly become a wonderland populated by a variety of denizens with multiple personalities (some might even say multiple personality disorders). Mountain biking is an integral part of our modern identities, transcending generations, income levels, geographic boundaries, and physical capabilities. It is a vehicle for competition, commerce, artistic expression, fashion, friendly association, and pilgrimage.

Mountain biking's original tribal gatherings took place on Marin County's legendary Repack course with riders bombing downhill in flannel shirts, Levis, and hiking boots. In the 1970s, downhill clunking was still trying to become a sport, and its practitioners were more a community than a culture. The Repack tradition survives some two decades later, if only for riders to ponder the pervasive hype, commercialization, social conflicts, and cycling prowess that have evolved in the wake of their engineering.

Given the nature of its origin, when the European road bike met the western wilderness, it was perhaps not surprising that racing became a dominant force in fat tire culture. This is epitomized every summer at Mammoth Mountain, in California's eastern Sierra Nevada, where twenty thousand riders and spectators journey to participate in and watch downhill and cross-country races. The faithful also congregate at a high-tech swap meet in the pits and expo areas maintained by bike companies and pro race teams, and attend parties where they can rub shoulders with world champions. Mountain bike culture is accessible, and whether you're a first-timer or a gold medalist, if you

While the advent of full suspension has taken the
mountain bike into more extreme downhill
environments, the classic clunker is still one of the
most fun and soulful ways of getting around town.

ride, you're part of the club. The industry's annual trade show, Interbike, takes place every autumn in the shadow of Disneyland. For four days dealers wander amidst the most beautiful and costly equipment on the planet, cutting deals on everything from tiny bike-shop orders to superstar race contracts. The show floor, the hotels, and the bars all overflow with bike folk during the event.

Like any real culture, off-roading is in a constant state of metamorphosis. The pioneers had an independent spirit. Joe Breeze, Gary Fisher, Tom Ritchey, Charlie Cunningham, Chris Chance, Scot Nicol, and others were consummate rider/inventors who built bikes first because they rode them. The money (and for some lots of it) came later. By the end of the 1980s, a new breed of high-performance technical masters was on the rise, and the rider/builders seemed to fade into the background. Superstar rider John Tomac typifies this second wave: smooth, dominant, professional, and rich. John Parker, whose Yeti Cycles broke both technical and stylistic ground, was the ultimate superstar builder. The Yeti had the image of a Ferrari: high-tech and expensive. With unconventional cable routing, oval tubing, and full suspension, Yeti established the prototype for bikes that were about pure, unadulterated speed. The race teams Parker assembled were so good they were often cherry-picked for talent by better-funded corporate outfits. Parker also helped lead the migration of the off-road community to the mountain bike mecca of Durango, Colorado, when he moved his company there from Southern California in the early 1990s.

Those second wavers have themselves been elbowed aside by an even newer school, typified by downhiller Shaun Palmer. A multisport athlete who began his

PROFESSIONAL RACERS HAVE ALWAYS HAD TO LOOK A CERTAIN WAY, WEARING COSTUMES THAT RESEMBLE A CROSS BETWEEN AN ANTHROPOMORPHIC BILLBOARD AND A COMIC-BOOK SUPERHERO.

career as a pro snowboarder, Palmer joined mountain biking not just because he was good at it, but because it fit his style. Mountain biking, as time goes on, has become less influenced by off-roading's original ancestors—clunking, road-bike racing, and motorcycling—and more by extreme sports like skateboarding, surfing, and snowboarding. We can only expect more of this cross-pollination.

The athleticism of the racers seems to intensify continually. As crowds swell, multinational conglomerates like Toyota, Mountain Dew, and Volkswagen sponsor teams, but the competitive spirit remains constant. It was thrilling when cross-country legend Joe Murray finished fourth at the Rock Hopper in 1983 wearing hiking sneakers and using no toe clips, on his way to NORBA National Championship wins in 1984 and 1985; or when Cindy Whitehead emerged victorious at the 1986 Sierra 7500, standing up over forty-nine miles of rigorous climbing and descending after her seat post snapped during the first mile of the race. It remains astonishing that Ned Overend, the sport's iron man at over forty, was still thrashing opponents in 1997 the way he did more than a decade earlier.

American dominance of off-road competition effectively ended in the mid-1990s with the emergence of strong riders, like Swiss cross-country specialist Thomas Frischknecht, French downhiller Nico Vouilloz, and Dutch world champion and 1996 Olympic gold medalist Bart Brentjens, from countries with long-established road-bike racing traditions. The Europeans, with their organized youth racing programs, have increased the level of competition; but they have changed the nature of off-road racing as well. Downhills are more challenging to accommodate the French daredevils. Cross-country events are

The Golden Gate
Bridge connects
San Francisco
riders with
recreation areas
that radiate
northward for
nearly twenty-
five miles,
making this one
of the best cities
for the sport.

Mounted Police

Though the Berkeley, California, Police Department can date its use of bicycles back to the beginning of the century, the official bicycle patrol program began in 1991 with two enthusiastic officers and a grant from the Bay Area Air Quality Control District. By 1997, thirteen full-time patrol officers were navigating their Trek, Bridgestone, and Cannondale front-suspension mountain bikes through the downtown and residential streets of Berkeley, claiming that the program has brought increased morale and better fitness to the department.

Locals concur that an officer astride a bicycle is both more accessible than one in a patrol vehicle and more responsive than one on foot. In the course of their training, bike patrol officers learn about safety, balance, and basic bike-handling skills, such as how to ride down a flight of stairs, hop curbs, maneuver through crowds, and dismount during a pursuit.

"Chasing pedestrians is always fun," says officer Mark Bachman, one of the pioneers of the program. Also popular is the stealth afforded by the bicycle approach. "I've burned my fingers so many times, sneaking up on people and grabbing the lit crack pipe out of their hands," Bachman adds.

According to the Seattle Police Department, which first re-introduced the concept of police biking, an officer on a bicycle has contact with five times as many people as a beat cop, and twenty times as many as an officer in a patrol car.

Many cities, such as San Francisco, whose police department is featured in the photo at left, have since mounted their officers on fat tire bikes.

held at lower altitudes and staged closer to urban areas to garner larger crowds.

Every year, more outstanding women riders are capturing a larger share of the attention of professional racing. Though men still earn more money, and there are more of them on the race circuit, the women have clearly proven they are as capable of high-speed competition. Missy Giove is arguably the sport's most exciting downhiller, and not just because of her body piercings, her braids, and the shriveled piranha around her neck. Watching Giove race is like witnessing an explosion. She's a sixty-mile-per-hour bullet.

Cross-country specialist Susan DeMattei retired in 1996 after winning the bronze for the U.S. Olympic team. DeMattei was bested by gold medalist Paola Pezzo, an exceptional athlete who took the gold for Italy in Mediterranean style: sexy, baring cleavage, wearing bright metallic shorts. Pezzo went on to win both the World Cup and World Championship in 1997.

Most immortal among women racers is Juli Furtado, who won seventeen major events in a row in 1993—the longest winning streak in off-road history—and single-handedly brought the women's side of the sport to a level that surpassed the men's pack in terms of excitement and tension. Furtado may be the greatest mountain bike racer ever; she certainly competes with Tomac and Overend for that title. After her streak, she competed for two seasons with mysteriously poor results. She was finally diagnosed with lupus, a life-threatening immune disorder, in 1997, and retired. Furtado was a strategic competitor who shined on both cross-country and downhill. Her early departure stands as one of the sport's most abbreviated chapters.

Today's racers work on two levels, as fitness deities and pop idols. Because off-road biking is so demanding, this isn't always a comfortable arrangement, but in most cases it pays the rent. "I sometimes wonder if it's me or the beard," confessed super-stylish rider Travis Brown, who is routinely consulted by mainstream bike magazines for his choices in records (alternative rock) and footwear (Doc Martens).

Professional racers have always had to look a certain way, wearing costumes that are a cross between an anthropomorphic billboard and a comic-book superhero. Former world downhill champ Greg Herbold found himself in the fortunate position of having a lifelong sponsor—Miyata—whose unfortunate signature color was pink, making him a poster-boy for mountain biking's neon era. "I'd be the first to admit there were times I looked hideous," he said.

Every culture has its fashion, and for years everyday trail jockeys dressed to the same trends. They went from flannel to fluorescent Lycra with hideous results, especially for hikers and small children who happened to see them flashing by on the trails. The "be an advertisement" era began a long halting skid in 1994, however, when San Francisco rider Tim Parr founded Swobo Clothing, a company dedicated to the simple proposition that bike clothes didn't have to look or feel goofy. Dozens of companies adopted that philosophy over the next

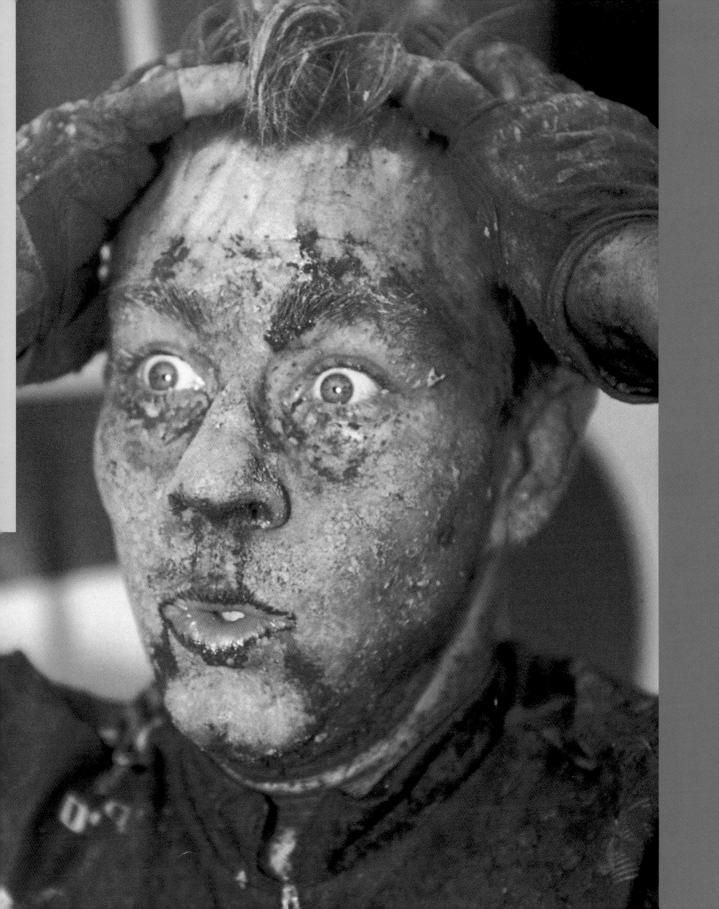

AIR: SPACE BETWEEN THE TIRES AND THE GROUND. BOTH TIRES MUST BE OFF THE GROUND, OR IT ISN'T AIR.

few years, and the "leisure wear" category was born. Lycra's death knell finally sounded in 1997, when a Southern California company called Nema introduced the ultimate in leisure wear, non-form-fitting bike shorts that were actually comfortable and good-looking.

While racers remain influential, bike companies have also begun to question, for the first time since the early days, whether spending big bucks on racing teams actually attracts new riders to the sport. Stealing a cue from snowboard makers, they've invented a new category called Freeriding. The Freeriders share many of the stereotypical attributes that have characterized their snow-surfing counterparts: a rebellious spirit, the lure of extreme vertical descents, and a propensity for grunge culture. Skeptics, on the other hand, view this as a marketing strategy (the term has been copyrighted by Cannondale) that makes it easier to sell the full-suspension bikes requisite for radical downhilling. Though the bike companies would have riders think that being one of these super-cool, super-stoked, super-soulful bikers requires a huge equipment investment, the truth is it merely requires a sense of passion and discipline that translates into a deep and abiding hunger for dirt.

Among mountain biking's arguably more sensible subcultures is the retro-grouch movement. A label originally cast by a magazine writer toward former Bridgestone U.S.A. product director Grant Peterson, retro-grouches began to question the mania for innovation overtaking the industry. "Bikes are just going the same route of golf drivers with big heads and oversized tennis rackets," says Peterson. "How else do you sell gear to people who already have perfectly functional bikes? Sweeping technological changes that by hook or by crook force out the old and bring in the new."

While many people argue that the newer bikes do in fact ride better, Peterson's and other retro-grouches' approach to cycling may be based more upon frugality, technological simplicity, and self-reliance than nostalgia or neo-Luddite posturing. Parts should be easy to maintain, they believe; frames should be lightweight yet durable; and more gears aren't necessarily better. Bound by their propensity to question every successive "advancement," a growing number of bike builders, whether they call themselves retro-grouches or not, are arguing for innovation only when appropriate. Peterson later founded Rivendell, a mail order and bike building outfit based in Northern California that specializes in traditional steel frames as well as hard-to-find classic components and accessories. The products are advertised in an excellent publication, *The Rivendell Reader*.

Jacquie Phelan is another prominent spirit arguing for less emphasis not just on technological gadgetry, but on testosterone and blood and guts. From 1981 to 1986, she was the women's national champion, but was known as much for her wacky antics as her outstanding riding skills. Phelan entered races under the pseudonym Alice B. Toeclips, posed for a RockShox ad wearing only mud and a feather, advocated for equal pay among women racers, and became a spokesperson for proper trail etiquette. As a contributing essayist to *Bike Magazine*, she has also

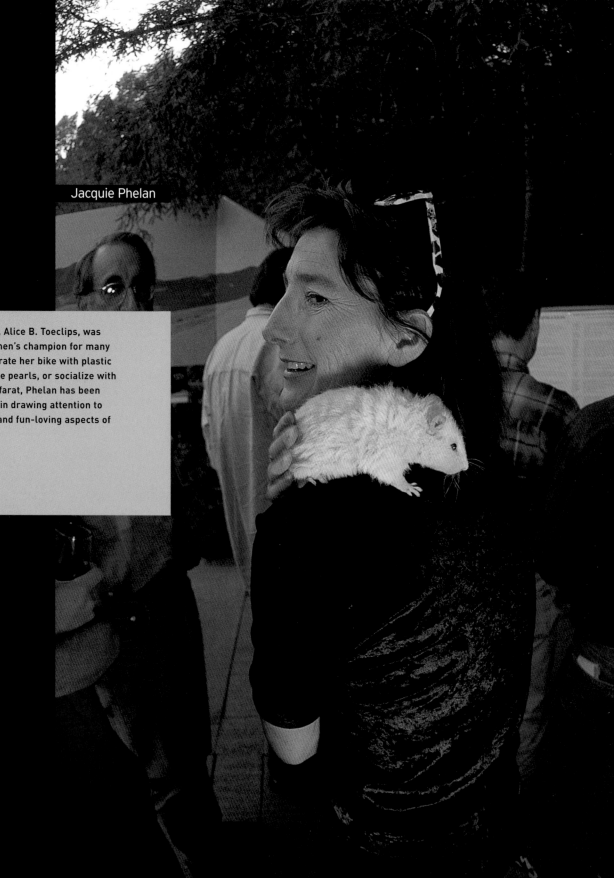

Jacquie Phelan

Jacquie Phelan, a.k.a. Alice B. Toeclips, was mounain biking's women's champion for many years. Known to decorate her bike with plastic flowers, race with fake pearls, or socialize with her pet rat Yassir Halfarat, Phelan has been extremely influential in drawing attention to both the competitive and fun-loving aspects of the sport.

Paola Pezzo

WOMEN RACERS TURNED IN RIVETING PERFORMANCES IN MOUNTAIN BIKING'S DEBUT AT THE 1996 ATLANTA GAMES.

Susan DeMattei

U.S. women riders thrived during the 1990s. From left to right: Ruthie Mathis, Susan DeMattei, Juli Furtado, and Tammy Jacques-Grewal. Mathis's many accomplishments include a World Championship victory. DeMattei went on to win the bronze medal in the Atlanta Olympic Games in 1996. Furtado's winning streak of seventeen consecutive major races in 1993 remains a record among men's and women's competitors. Jacques-Grewal is a talented racer in her own right.

SKY YAEGER

Sky Yaeger is one female bike-industry professional who doesn't spend a lot of time worrying about gender inequities in mountain biking. Now a product manager for Bianchi U.S.A., Yaeger started working in a bike shop in 1972, earned three art degrees, and eventually became a self-described bike bum.

"Considering my art background, I probably should have gone into the advertising side of the business," says Yaeger, "but I happen to be interested in cars, bikes, and tools.

"I find myself in the world of technology, because that is what a large part of cycling is about," she says. "Some things appeal to males more than females, and technology is one of those things. But I don't think we're failing as an industry because there aren't more female bike designers out there."

Though Yaeger claims not to be interested at all in clothes or shopping, she does admit to stashing a pair of Bianchi Celeste green pumps underneath her desk and regrets being bested at the inaugural costume party at the Moab Fat Tire Festival by a guy with a toilet seat on his head.

Sky Yaeger

contributed her fair share of philosophical wanderings and humor to the bike world. Perhaps Phelan's most influential contribution was the establishment of the Women's Mountain Bike* Tea Society (the star is intentional), otherwise known as the WOMBATS, an organization she founded in 1986 as a way to attract her fellow sisters to her beloved sport. The name combines the daintiness of a Victorian women's club with the thrills of mountain biking. Phelan's 1998 web page reads:

"We uppity WOMBATS are staking out some gals-only territory on the outskirts of the 'gnarly' sport of mountain biking, and it is quite an adventure. We believe that the more women ride, the less likely the Sierra Club will be able to portray off-road cyclists as testosterone-poisoned youth in search of destruction. We will get these energetic guys to maintain trails with us, then make 'em go race so they can shred without guilt, while we: a) get ready for our own race, b) sit on the sidelines cheering, c) get our girlfriends to do a three-hour ride instead of watching a dumb 'ol race, d) write a letter to our congressperson asking for more money for bike projects, e) stay home and relax—the kids are with dad on their bikes."

Yet another label to mushroom under the fat tire umbrella is the "soul rider." These are not necessarily downhillers or singletrackers or racers. They may be families, like the Maedas, of Altadena, California—seven of them at last count, ranging from eleven-year-old Zak to Grandpa Sam, age sixty-nine. Or they may be messengers, like San Francisco courier Jason Makapagal, whose simple philosophy is to ride "like they can't see you. Because they can't." Or they may be regular guys like Ed and Kyle Cashen, personal trainers from New York who destroy bikes routinely, and who, when their rigs fail, often run for the rest of the race and usually finish in the top ten anyway. They're Mark DeVries, who works all summer long laying railroad ties in Northern Canada—his crew can place as many as ten thousand ties a day—and still finds the energy to ride after work and convince his buddies to try it, too.

The Laguna Rads, a
Southern California-
based group of
extreme riders.

Mountain biking is no longer limited to wealthy, industrialized nations. One soul rider, for example, who calls himself Chu-Chu, rides trails in the Venezuelan Andes, from the top of sixteen thousand-foot peaks to the Caribbean, a hundred miles below. Then there is the Ibarra family of Mexico City, which is entirely employed in the industry. One owns a bike shop, one is a pro racer, and another is the country's premier trail guide.

At the other end of the spectrum from soul riding lies the temple of (testosterone and) technology worship. This locus was exemplified at Interbike 1995, where the hit of the event was Alex Pong, who showed off a Cannondale concept bike called the "Magic" that got gullible techno-freaks salivating. It was glitzy and flash, it was expensive, and it was revolutionary and futuristic, but it was merely a prototype with no chance of mass production.

The next year, understanding that if you're going to produce flash you might as well put it in a bikini, many companies abandoned wide-eyed technological hype in favor of old-fashioned advertising. Cannondale's booth drew bigger, leering crowds with a sexy aerobic dance show. A year later, Cannondale combined the two approaches when it debuted the Raven, a spiritual descendent of Pong's Magic (which by then was actually in production) and also kept the sex parade.

The mountain bike explosion has also given birth to an international publishing boom. In the United States, there are a number of continuously published off-road mags, including *Mountain Bike*, *Mountain Bike Action*, *Bike*, *Dirt Rag*, *Mountain Biking*, and *Mountain Biker*. In addition, there are *Bicycling* magazine, a general interest publication, and *Velo-News*, which covers bike racing. *Mountain Bike Action* acts as the industry's technological trade magazine, if you define the industry narrowly as located in Southern California. *Mountain Bike*, with the biggest circulation, cuts right down the

ONLY IN A TENT AS BIG AS MOUNTAIN BIKING COULD SO MANY DISPARATE GROUPS FIND COMMON GROUND.

Single-Speed Racing

Every influence that has pushed off-roading forward technologically—suspension, aluminum alloys, advanced shifting—seems to be matched by an opposite if not equal reaction. The latest in off-road hardcore entails abandoning derailleurs and shifters altogether for single-speed bikes.

A single-speed bike requires a fixed-gear rear cog, usually with 16, 17, or 18 teeth, and a 44- or 46-tooth front chainring. Specially-built frames, with horizontal dropouts so the chain can be tensioned properly, are better, but you can rig one by adding a derailleur or downhill chain tensioner to keep the chain tight, too. Other trick items like suspension and V or disc brakes are acceptable, but the drivetrain must be simple.

What's cool about these bikes? The degree of difficulty is formidable. No gears means there are neither super-low cogs to grind up the hills on nor big-ring torque for downhilling. What you get, though, is pure simplicity, with surprisingly good performance. If anything, riding and racing a single-speed reminds one of how much can be done with limited technology.

Single-speed is an emerging race category, too. In the early days, there was a single-speed off-road national championship—the first was won by downhill legend Greg Herbold. At the 1997 24 Hours of Moab event, twenty racers competed on single-speeds. In Northern California today, the California Crusty Cruiser Cup is open only to single-speed riders.

middle of the path and appeals to everyday riders with products, stories, tips, and columns. *Bike* aims for the soul-rider contingent and avoids the equipment focus of the others but emphasizes gorgeous pictures and elegant layout. *Dirt Rag* is a growing zine that concentrates on the East Coast, and, in a brilliant strategic move, includes microbrew reviews.

Mountain Bike Action and *Mountain Bike* also share another thing: editor Zapata Espinoza. This aggressive, obsessive member of the Mountain Bike Hall of Fame started at *MBA*—bringing it to number one—and then overtook his old magazine when he switched to *Mountain Bike* in 1993. Love him or hate him, Espinoza (a.k.a. Zap) is one of the sport's influential personalities, not because he's a great rider, but because he's acted, throughout his career, as an odd, controversial, and surprising bridge between the average rider and the bike industry.

When Espinoza prints a negative review of a part, a manufacturing technique, or a whole company, it can become cause for panic, alarm, and consultations with lawyers. When something strikes his fancy, however, it's the Midas touch. His relationship with Yeti, for example, led to that company's elevation as the premier race rig of the early 1990s.

Because there is so much competition, off-road journalism is a fierce enterprise. Battles over exclusive tests on the hottest bikes are common; so are vendettas against companies that try to favor one magazine over another. There is a constant tug of war and a continuous battle for advertising dollars. Each magazine tries to represent its mix as the best and, to a lesser extent, believes that the others are missing the boat when it comes to serving real riders.

While mountain biking remains an information-intensive sport—people are always wondering where and what to ride—the next wave of off-road journalism may be in the world of computers, not print. There are already hundreds of websites devoted to mountain bikes, ranging from sites run by the magazines to web zines that offer alternatives to the glossy publications. Many of the sites are the labor of individuals who just want to tell you what the trails are like near their homes.

Only in a tent as big as mountain biking could so many disparate groups find common ground. Only a mountain bike can replace, comfortably, both a Harley Davidson and an ox. Some riders see the off-road world as getting too diverse and potentially splintering. There's the ride-up-the-mountain contingent, which views the summer chairlift riders as lazy sell-outs. There are the thousands who crowd the Slickrock Trail, outside Moab, while just one or two riders a day show up on the Kokopelli Trail, only a few miles away and equally as rewarding. Some like to belong, others thrive on being iconoclasts. As off-roading approaches the new millennium, these differences have overtaken the old arguments about which technology is better or appropriate.

Generally speaking, many of the pioneers who created the industry's greatest crest of sales and innovation in the 1980s are now in their mid-thirties. Many are married, have kids, and are learning to kick back a little. The younger guys are getting more radical, not just with their tatoos and body piercings, but also with horrifying orthopedic contraptions to hold their bones in place after many accidents.

Mountain biking really has become a culture. It's not just a gadget freak's hobby. It's not just about competition, but a way of life that holds together very different kinds of people who share a love of riding. At its center is an amazing machine, powered by adventurous people, that in this world of eighty-hour work weeks, traffic jams, and rampaging development, gets people into nature faster, better, cleaner, and easier than anything ever invented before it.

VICTOR VINCENTE OF AMERICA

Victor Vincente of America (yes, that's his name) is a fairly grizzled and somewhat familiar figure to riders around the Santa Monica Mountains, outside Los Angeles. Vincente was born Michael Hiltner, and he has major bike credentials: he was on two U.S. Olympic teams, and he holds the double transcontinental record (thirty-six days, eight hours), which he set in 1975.

It was on that ride that Victor Vincente of America was born. "I took on the name as a title commemorating my successful completion of that record-establishing ride," he says. "Not long after that, I discovered dirt roads."

Vincente isn't kidding when he uses the word *discovered*. He built his first "VVA" bikes in the late 1970s, dedicating them to Topanga Canyon, the hideaway that blossomed between Los Angeles and Malibu during the post-hippie period.

At that time Vincente also began writing his masterpiece, a still-in-progress epic poem about a mountain biker's struggles and discoveries. Subscribers to the sporadically published *Topanga Rider's Bulletin* were treated, whenever the mood struck Vincente, to the off-road equivalent of Milton.

"I wanted to put some of my experiences down on paper," he says, "so I came up

Victor Vincente of America

with the format: the focal point would be a bike rider, a fictitious bike rider, and he'd be going through some place I'd been, or some place I'd dreamed up. Some of the events described were real, others were more or less fictional."

While Vincente's poetry isn't exactly the kind academics might award genius grants to, there's a certain charm—and a definite passion—to his work. "I find my mind is mine, I imagined I saw a hole in my mind, it was difficult to comprehend, I thought I saw a hole in my mind," he wrote in his 1991 "Selected Verses and Art" chapbook, which collected his writing.

Despite his creative powers, his technical prowess, and his physical achievements, Vincente is probably best known for his culinary talents, specifically his recipe for road kill jerky. This is serious business; it's not just about a quick snack in the wild.

"I was up on the north end of Topanga Canyon," he recalls, "and I came across the owl. It was mostly eaten, but there were wings and a little breast meat. That became the famous owl jerky. It's my version of a Powerbar. Wild animals are the ultimate power food; I think that consuming creatures has an effect. When I eat them, I'm remembering their spirit. I'm consuming the traces of their spiritual experience."

SWOBO

Tim Parr

Tim Parr is the kind of guy who probably stole the cardigan sweaters out of his dad's closet, wore them while riding to school on his skateboard, and managed to pull it off with nary a funny look. It's this sort of thinking that incited Parr to start Swobo Clothing. Swobo style is an amalgamation of old-school and new, reuniting a classic fabric—wool—with the functionality required by the present day. The 100% merino wool cycling clothes are warm yet breathable, lightweight yet enduring; they won't stink when you sweat in them, and yet they are fully washable. And for those equally as likely to be caught sashaying across a crowded dance floor as navigating a hairy singletrack, Parr has also created a line of action leisure wear.

Swobo's influence on the bicycle—not to mention fashion—industry is reflected in the range of its wearers, whom the company describes as "prodigy altar boys, limo drivers all jacked up on bee pollen and royal jelly, and alien abductees." It is also epitomized by Swobo's novel approach to commercial publicity, such as Parr's appearances at bike races and industry events with cases of cheap beer and a posse of professional sideline hecklers.

Since Parr grew up participating in many of the anti-establishment sports that have now become industry mainstays, like surfing, skateboarding, and snowboarding, why choose the bicycle industry (in which, until recently, the phrase bicycle fashion might have been considered an oxymoron) on which to inflict his particular sensibilities? In true Swobo style, it was the challenge Parr saw in the opportunity to break the rules.

THE "BE AN ADVERTISEMENT" ERA BEGAN A LONG HALTING SKID IN 1994, WHEN SAN FRANCISCO RIDER TIM PARR FOUNDED SWOBO.

The Bicycle Messenger

Although many of them don't ride typical mountain bikes as part of their daily routine, no group has defined the rebellious nature of modern cycling culture more than bicycle messengers. Out in the streets, facing almost universal contempt, messengers battle for asphalt real estate and respect from machines that outweigh them several hundred times. They are often paid per delivery rather than at an hourly rate, and they are besieged at every turn by cars, buses, streetcars, police, and even pedestrians.

The messenger life is one of speed, violence, and uncertainty; and because it is a life on the margins, it yields an incredible outpouring of expression and culture. From the most basic idioms of dress and language to the more complex vocabulary of music and painting, the messenger scene possesses its own distinct and vital heartbeat. Once a year, the bike couriers of the world gather to celebrate their community at the Cycle Messenger World Championships. First held in 1993 in Berlin, the event isn't so much a race as it is a frolic. When CMWC invaded San Francisco at the end of summer in 1996, the art shows, bands, bike tours, and nightly parties were at least as important as the competitions, which included trials, cargo bike races, sprint events, and a best bike contest.

In compact, messenger-heavy cities such as New York, Boston, Washington, D.C., San Francisco, Seattle, and Vancouver, the couriers are the most high-profile cyclists in their communities, encountered daily by every side of society. As a result, they are often a flash point for bike-related issues. Critical Mass, a monthly protest aimed to garner more rights for the bicycle as a legitimate and essential form of urban transportation, was founded by a group of messengers in San Francisco in 1993. Today Critical Mass is held monthly in over a dozen cities and has had a major influence on the bicycle policies of many of America's largest metropolitan areas.

NO GROUP HAS
MORE DEFINED
THE REBELLIOUS
NATURE
OF MODERN
CYCLING
CULTURE THAN
BICYCLE
MESSENGERS.

PIRATE

bike
MAGAZINE

RUSHed

International Alleycat Review

"PART OF THE ATTRACTION OF BEING A COURIER ARE THOSE MOMENTS OF PURE ...DANGER... ADRENALINE."

Buffalo Bill,
Moving Target

Way Out Zines

To document the messenger universe, an entire array of fanzines and comic books has emerged. Sporadically published magazines from urban centers in the United States such as *Dead Air* (Chicago), *Iron Lung* (Seattle), *Cars on the Velodrome* (Philadelphia), and *Bicycle Siren* (San Francisco) have been joined by even more obscure publications from around the world like *Hideous White Noise*, out of Toronto, Canada, and *Mr. Nice Guy*, from Sydney, Australia. All chronicle the plight of the messenger: frequent injuries, no health insurance, and low pay. *Moving Target,* with some twenty-three issues since 1988, claims to be the oldest messenger zine in the world. Described by its publisher, known only as Buffalo Bill, as the voice of the international messenger community, *Moving Target* is a savage satire of the messenger life. *Messenger 29*, a comic started by New York bike mechanic Jay Jones, details the life of a masked messenger superhero who fights for good (good in the eyes of a messenger) on the streets of Gotham.

Sculpture commissioned for the 1994 London Cycle Messenger World Championship, dedicated to all messengers killed while on the job.

ONCE A YEAR THE BIKE COURIERS
OF THE WORLD GATHER TO
CELEBRATE THEIR COMMUNITY AT
THE CYCLE MESSENGER WORLD
CHAMPIONSHIPS.

Racing

Mountain bike races began to spring up in the mid-1970s in various pockets of California and Colorado. Races like the Repack downhill, thirty miles north of San Francisco, and the Puerco Canyon Downhill, which soared above the sea in Malibu, sparked the competitive fires of many of the sport's early founders. Just as bicycle road racing has been shaped by its European roots, mountain bike racing has always been known for a particularly American flair. Defined from its earliest days by the principles of fun and adventure, it has always attracted a breed of individual less interested in team sports, conformity, and daily routine.

Over the years, larger races—such as the international Grundig/UCI World Cup and National Off-Road Bicycling Association (NORBA) series races— have garnered the lion's share of the limelight and sponsorship dollars. But the smaller events still preserve the adventurous soul of fat tire racing.

Even as huge events with high entry fees and less-than-challenging loop courses have attracted massive crowds, off-beat races still thrive in the heart of the racing community. The Leadville 100 is a torturous hundred-mile epic around the high-altitude mountain town of Leadville, Colorado. The course never dips below an altitude of ten thousand feet and takes even the best riders over seven hours to complete. The 24 Hours of Canaan, held in West Virginia every May since 1995, and its sister race in Moab, Utah, are team endurance events that start at noon on a Saturday and continue through the night until noon the next day. Teams of four or five riders compete, relay style, battling bitter cold conditions and darkness at night.

Mountain bikers compete in a range of categories, including Beginner, Sport, Expert, Semi-Pro, and Pro. In addition to men's and women's divisions, age brackets further define the pack: junior (18 and under), senior (19-34), veteran (35-44), and master (45 and up).

Like many sports, mountain biking has both a World Cup and World Championship. The World Cup is a season-long worldwide series spanning four continents. The World Championship is a one-day race at season's end. Both are sanctioned by Union Cyclistes International (UCI) and sponsored by the German stereo and communications manufacturer Grundig.

The big money in racing these days is in downhilling—though television coverage is spotty. ESPN's X-Games is the only event with a regularly scheduled downhill component. Even so, racers like Shaun Palmer, Mike King, Nico Vouilloz, and Missy Giove are commanding salaries that often run into the mid-six-figures. This is not an astonishing amount in the context of mainstream professional sports, but it indicates a tremendous advance from the days when pioneer racers competed for nothing more than the thrill of it.

North American Bicycle Association (NORBA) events—held in the United States—helped to establish mountain bike racing in the sport's early years. The growth of the sport through international events like the World Cup and World Championships has greatly increased the quantity and quality of competition.

"RACING IS A **365** DAY PER YEAR JOB AND **24** HOURS A DAY. YOU DON'T JUST GO HOME AND DO WHATEVER YOU WANT AT THE END OF THE DAY."

Thomas Frischknecht

INTERVIEWS

Even though mountain bike pros occupy the elite stratospheres of physical ability and stardom, they are a lot like regular mountain bike riders in that they have chosen to ride bikes because they are passionate about the sport. The money can be good for the few who are the world's best, but it never approaches the salary of even the lowest-level NBA star, whose degree of athleticism the best off-roaders easily match. We've chosen to feature some of the most successful and dynamic racers in the history of mountain biking. There are others, of course, but the achievements and personalities of the individuals here have helped to color the sport.

Juli Furtado

JULI FURTADO
CROSS COUNTRY WORLD CHAMPION AND WORLD CUP CHAMPION

Juli Furtado came to mountain biking after knee operations cut short a promising ski-racing career. She proceeded to leave a legacy as mountain biking's most gifted racer. Winning a record seventeen consecutive major races in 1993, she dominated the women's circuit between 1992 and 1995, earning the title of Queen Juli. Furtado's race results were frequently competitive with the top-place finishers in the expert men's category, and significantly raised the standards of achievement for a new generation of women racers.

In a 1998 *Velo News* tribute, Furtado's close competitor Susan DeMattei said, "I have a contention that people who grew up skiing . . . have a little more savvy with their technical riding; they know how to pick a line at high speeds—and Julie definitely knew how to do that. She wasn't afraid to get hurt and she certainly wasn't afraid of speed."

Though her goals were set on Olympic ski competition, mountain biking took her to the Atlanta Games in 1996. By that time, however, she was beginning to suffer from the debilitating symptoms of the autoimmune deficiency disease lupus erythematosis, and finished tenth. Now retired, Furtado explains, "I don't have to go out for three hours—I can go for an hour and it's fine. I'm realizing how good it is for me. I think I would have been a mountain biker even if I wasn't a pro athlete, because I really do love the sport."

Missy Giove

MISSY GIOVE
WORLD DOWNHILL CHAMPION

Missy Giove is off-roading's most recognizable face. The 1996 Grundig World Cup overall downhill champion and 1994 world champion, Giove epitomizes, at least outwardly, the sport's wild, extreme side. She is heavily pierced and funkily coifed, and she talks a mile a minute. Giove is one of the sport's most thoughtful and spiritual riders; she has a deep sense of commitment to bringing others, especially women, into the mountain bike arena.

"Mountain biking is my religion. For me it's an expression of who I am, what my purpose is. It's not to mountain bike, it's to inspire people. It really helps me with my connection with myself, and other people in the world, in the universe. I love it, and I love the peacefulness of it; and sometimes the on-the-edge screaming part of it, too.

"To me, mountain bike culture is about people who love the sport, really feel inspired by it, and take it to other parts of their life; people who appreciate their connection with nature and explore themselves through biking.

"I'm a racer because I like to push my limits and see how good I can become. It's a way to have a scale, to see where I'm at. Racing really pushes me toward finding my maximum, and I like that. The other reason I'm a racer is I like to share my passion for mountain biking with others. I get to share my story with the public and hopefully inspire someone."

NED OVEREND
CROSS COUNTRY WORLD CUP AND WORLD CHAMPION

Ned Overend is the world's winningest off-road racer. He retired at age forty to become coach of the Specialized team, but Overend continues to race, just for "fun." Overend's definition of fun is contending and always being a threat to win against riders who are half his age.

"I'll probably continue to compete at some level into my old age," says the former 1990 world champion and six-time national champion. "I'm really interested in being fit, pushing my limits; I like the rush of going fast through the trees. The excitement of it all. The other reason I'll stay so involved is that I'm kind of a gear freak. I like to help develop products. Part of my continuing to race is justified by testing new products in competition."

An athlete who was accomplished at a number of sports, Overend found mountain biking tied together all of his skills. "It used my climbing and crossover technical skills. The personalities in mountain biking also jibed better with me than in the road bike scene. People seemed to be in the sport because they enjoyed riding in the back country."

Perhaps Overend's most significant contributions to fat tire culture have been his approachable, low-key personality combined with a physical endurance that has kept him competitive. "I hope I've made the sport less intimidating to people," he says. "I've tried to have an attitude that I'm not special."

Ned Overend

Bob Rol

BOB ROLL
6-TIME TOUR DE FRANCE FINISHER; PROFESSIONAL OFF-ROAD RACER

Bob Roll is the James Joyce of off-roading. While he has been both a professional road racer (riding in the Tour de France) and an off-road racer, perhaps his greatest contribution has been writing and philosophizing about the sport in his various articles that have appeared in *Velo News*, in the on-line magazine *Charged*, and elsewhere.

In one of his signature stream-of-consciousness columns for *Charged*, Roll writes, "You, too, can regain the floating equilibrium of your womb origins. Go out to the trails. Get down on your hands and knees and feel the soil, smell it, run your fingers and toes through it. Divine intervention will come and, like me, you will transcend the constraints modern living imposes on every post-aquatic human embryo." More than anyone, Roll illuminates the joy—and the suffering—pro riders go through on the circuit.

"For me, mountain biking is a religion, but it's a personal convention," he says. "It's not limited to the conventions of a bunch of edicts and rules. I make it up as I go along. I couldn't live without biking. You know when Michelangelo painted the Sistine Chapel? For me it's carving up singletrack—I approach it the same way.

"Mountain bike culture is really spread out," says Roll, a committed racer who sees the sport as definitely more individual- than team-oriented. "It isn't a roving circus like the Grateful Dead was; it's a lot more random than that. You have to look harder for the sublime moments of consciousness. You can have a Pedro's Festival on one hand and a NORBA championship on the other, and rarely do the twain meet. When they do it's pretty special—a melting pot of recreation riders, downhillers, cowboys, and police."

Thomas Frischknecht

THOMAS FRISCHKNECHT
'96 ATLANTA OLYMPIC GAMES, SILVER MEDALIST. MULTI-WORLD-CUP CHAMPION

"Even though it wasn't the gold, winning the silver medal in the 1996 Olympics in Atlanta was the biggest race and biggest success of my career," says Swiss cyclo-cross and mountain biker Thomas Frischknecht. "The whole world was watching and the pressure was on, because I was one of the favorites going into the race and I had been working really hard for that day for a long time. Then to come through and get where I wanted to be—the podium—it was a great satisfaction."

Now working toward the 2000 Games in Sydney, Frischknecht enjoys the enviable position of being a Team Ritchey rider and having Tom Ritchey as his personal tinkerer and mechanic. "I can call him up and talk to him about a tire design six months before a race and he'll have the prototype four months later."

Frischknecht, who has been with the Ritchey team throughout the 1990s and earned his fair share of world championships, in both the United States and in Europe, believes that professional racing is a total commitment. "It's a 365 day per year job and twenty-four hours a day. You don't just go home and do whatever you want at the end of the day. Success makes this the best job in the world. You get everything you want and you're really satisfied with what you're doing. On the other hand, it can be really disappointing when things aren't going well. You're assessed by your results, by second place finishes. Because you're judged by how you finish, it's really obvious how well you do."

The son of a professional racer, Frischknecht says the upper echelons of racing require not only physical discipline but mental prowess. "It's hard to say an exact percentage, but when you end up competing with the greatest talents in the world, you all have very good physical skills. What makes the difference is the ability to use these talents to win races."

John Stamstad

JOHN STAMSTAD
IDITASPORT EXTREME CHAMPION

Snow is not always an unwelcome occurrence at off-road events. The fluffy stuff defines the Iditasport Extreme, a human-powered slugfest held every February in Alaska. Riders follow the first and most difficult 350 miles of the Iditarod Sled Dog trail between Knik and McGrath: pushing, pedaling, and nearly swimming through deep snow, ice, and tire-clogging slush. Like Canaan, Iditasport is an event that rejects the corporate nature of modern off-road racing for a more rugged individualism. This is epitomized by Klondike Cruiser John Stamstad, the only rider who has won both events. Stamstad receives a special dispensation at the relay-team race at Canaan; they let him compete solo. Stamstad wrote this about the Iditasport Extreme:

"At one point I was pushing the bike up a hill, staring at my feet, when I heard a loud snort and saw a cow moose with calf charging, kicking at me. I retreated before she got to me (she got within a few feet), and we stared at each other from a relatively safe distance, while I worried about everybody catching me as I was blocked by the moose. Moose like these trails because the alternative is walking through six feet of deep snow. I tried yelling, and finally got real close and when she took one step off the trail, I sprinted for it. After fourteen hours of very hilly and bumpy riding I made it into Rainy Pass Lodge, 2.5 hours ahead of the next rider, Brian Toddeshini. . . .

A couple of miles before the checkpoint of Nickoli, I met two Athabaskan natives checking their trap lines. One offered me a Pepsi and I almost cried, I wanted it so bad. For the last thirty hours all I had thought about was drinking something carbonated. After leaving Nickoli, the finish line in McGrath is only fifty miles down river, but it's a long fifty. You get to a point where you can see the searchlight from the airport and you think the town must be just on the other side of the next hill. Two to three agonizing hours later you finally make it there. When I got off the bike I could barely walk. I felt perfect until the point when I realized that I had finished, and then my body just shut down. I could barely move. The next morning was minus twenty-five degrees Fahrenheit in McGrath. The race started on February 22. I finished five days, five hours later on the 27th."

Destinations

Off-roading's most holy sites have both history and currency. They are living communities, not museums.

Mountain Bike Meccas

MARIN COUNTY

Mount Tamalpais

Richmond

Angel Island

Marin Headlands

Sausalito

Alcatraz

San Francisco Bay

Pacific Ocean

San Francisco

Although singletracks have been closed for some time, Southern Marin County still offers mountain bikers a wide range of trails with varying degrees of vertical rise and duration. This map shows the mountainous terrain that rises between the Marin Headlands and Pine Mountain, north of Mt. Tam, where Repack originated.

Off-roading's most holy sites have both history and currency. They are living communities, not museums. Mt. Tam is where the sport was born, and where battles are still being waged over whether bikers should have access to certain hiking trails. While studies have shown that responsibly ridden bikes cause no more erosion than hiking, noncyclists have argued that encountering mountain bikers on trails threatens both their safety and their peace of mind—and they have exaggerated their concerns to the point of hysteria. Ironically, bikers have been banned from virtually all of Tam's singletracks for some time.

After nearly a decade of lobbying efforts failed to keep Mt. Tam trails open to cyclists, in 1994 frustrated activists began clandestine construction of New Paradigm, an illegal trail that attempted to prove that off-roading and single-track riding were not incompatible. New Paradigm was exceptionally well-built, with a hidden entrance. It dropped 1,100 feet in 2.1 miles, featuring gentle grades

and incessant switchbacks through thick woods. Upon its discovery by the local Marin Municipal Water District, however, the trail was destroyed by community conservation groups. While no longer ridden, the New Paradigm Trail has served as a catalyst within the mountain bike community for political organizing in the ongoing struggle to keep challenging and rewarding trails accessible.

No such problems exist in Durango, Colorado. This Rocky Mountain town gained popularity in the late 1980s as the residence of choice for the pros. Ned Overend had been a resident for years, and when racers John Tomac, Juli Furtado, and the Yeti Cycles company headquarters moved there, the secret about this high altitude rider's paradise became widely known. Today, nearly every major working pro calls Durango home. In the summer, the town's main street is jammed from end to end with off-roaders. Per capita bagel consumption has tripled since 1990. The reason is not just the trails. "It's that the trails are *open*," says pro Bob Roll, who has lived in Durango since 1990. "It's totally unrestricted." While many towns are closing trails to bikers, Durango continues to open new ones, an average of three per year.

Trails define an off-road mecca. In a way similar to how fishing holes are discovered, once a rider sets wheel to them and tells a few friends, a place's legend is born. The Kegeti Pass, for example, has become a proving ground for true adventurers. It is as remote as you can imagine, ten hours by bus from Bishkek, captial of Kyrgyzstan (formerly part of the Soviet Union). The Kegeti is part of the legendary Silk Road trade route, and riding it is now becoming a popular rite of passage among the hard-core world-traveler crowd. "It's a long, hard day's riding," says guide Jonathan Bobaljik. "Up the pass, over the top, and back down the other side. The summit is so covered in snow and ice that you have to walk. The total distance is about forty miles, which takes about ten hours."

DURANGO

Animas River

Durango

N E S W

Durango, Colorado, has become the residence of a great many of the sport's professional racers and recreational fanatics. The reason appears to be simple. For mountain bikers, quality of life has a direct correlation with trail access.

The fat tire bike is truly an all-terrain vehicle. Top left and right: Vancouver, British Columbia. Below: the Utah desert.

The sport of mountain biking is growing so rapidly worldwide that dozens of new "classic" trails are born each year. In Europe, the highly structured trail networks of tightly managed preserves have begun to welcome mountain bikers. In the south of France, *les vélos tout terrain* are establishing new destinations, such as the expansive Luberon National Park and Mt. Ventoux, which has a crippling downhill that serves as a training ground to many of the world's fastest riders. Europeans also attend mountain bike races in huge numbers. In 1994, a crowd estimated at over fifty thousand watched Leigh Donovan and Nico Vouilloz win the downhill world championships at Kirchzarten, Germany. Even more astonishing, the audience paid to get in.

The growth of towns known as off-road centers is being replicated in Europe as well. Italy's Lago di Garda, south of the Dolomites, is probably Europe's most developed off-road village, with dozens of trails, resident riders, and a friendly vibe that offers everything Durango does. Festivals are springing up in Eastern Europe as well. Turnov, in the Czech Republic, where a 1996 World Cup race was held, is angling to become another European Durango. In Spain, El Camino de Santiago is emerging as one of the continent's top off-road routes, with a twist. It follows the thousand-year-old path Gotescalco, the Bishop of Le Puy, used as he made his way from France to Santiago de Compostela. Gotescalco was beatified for his troubles. Mountain bikers just get tired.

Both European and American riders know that you're not a true off-roader unless you've visited Moab, Utah, probably the most legendary mountain bike destination on the planet. Though Moab has a history of attracting motorized off-road recreationists, the town nearly died after the uranium industry went bust twenty years ago. But Moab had another natural resource—slickrock, a type of smooth red stone that rises up all over the Canyonlands area. As a proper noun, Slickrock was a legendary motorbike trail just outside town. In

Word spread that Moab was even better than the photos. Not just the Slickrock, but other trails, like Poison Spider Mesa and Amasa Bac

Colorado River

Arches
Ntl Park

Moab

Slickrock
Trail

Colorado River

MOAB

If there is one destination that attracts more riders than any other, Moab, Utah, is now the prime contender. The slickrock formations characteristic of this part of the country, a number of which are open to mountain bikers, offer unique and challenging riding conditions. The smooth red rock that takes shape in domes, bowls, and plateaus has led many to compare it to what riding on the moon might be like.

the early 1980s, mountain bikers began to ride it, too. Many of them, without modern conveniences like suspension and decent brakes, emerged bloody and smiling. Word spread that Moab trails were mystical; not just Slickrock, but trails that navigate narrow paths and offer breathtaking views of the Canyonlands, like the dangerous and highly exposed Poison Spider Mesa, and the expansively gorgeous Amasa Back. By 1991, Moab had several bike shops, a fat tire festival, and new motels on Main Street. The advent of dual-suspension made Moab seemingly complete. With shock-absorbing bikes available for rent all over town, Slickrock has become a doable challenge for most riders, a thousand of whom ride daily during the peak season of late August through November. Not surprisingly, the ecological damage to the region's fragile soils from such intensive trail use has become increasingly apparent, and an education campaign is now underway to prevent ecosystem abuse. Riders are being diverted to optional local trails to lessen the impact.

Mammoth Mountain is the racing equivalent of Moab; it is legendary, and it has been remade by the mountain bike. Situated in the Sierra Nevada, Mammoth is

California's largest winter sports area, but it used to be a sleepy place after the snow melted. Bill Cockroft, an employee at the resort, decided to bring riders up the hill on the chairlift in summer, and send them hurtling at speeds up to sixty miles per hour down the rough-and-tumble snowcat trail. He called the run Kamikaze. And he staged the event around a fun-packed race weekend that included a cross-country segment, a hill climb, trials, and a dual slalom. The race, which debuted in 1985, is now a signature event in the world of extreme sports.

Racing at Mammoth set another important off-road precedent: accessibility. Mountain bike races are open to everyone. At Mammoth, anyone can compete on the same course a world champ rides on. Mammoth also defined the concept of the race expo, the open pit areas where regular riders mingle with the pros, ogling the latest in prototype equipment. Over ten thousand visitors show up the week the racers come to town, and on some busy summer weekends, Mammoth is almost as strewn with mountain bikers as it is with snowboarders during the winter. Several races now follow the Mammoth model, with egalitarian courses and high-profile expos. Traces of Cockroft's idea are found at Mt. Snow, in Vermont, and at the bike race world's annual season opener, the Cactus Cup, in Phoenix, Arizona.

East Coast off-road riding evolved differently. With fewer (and less steep) places to ride, riding there is about finesse, nature, and the woods. It took Gil Willis, of West Virginia's Elk River Touring Center, to combine the longhaired mellowness of the east with the fun and passion of a West Coast gathering of the faithful. Elk River's Fat Tire Festival usually happens in early August, and it still includes some of the hallmarks of a late 1980s off-road gathering, such as clinics, workshops, and a Huffy toss, where participants compete to see who can throw a junk bike the farthest. The festival model is also well-represented at Wisconsin's Chequamegon gathering, the oldest race east of the Mississippi, held every September, and Fat Tire Bike Week in

Crested Butte, Colorado. The sport's oldest running frolic, it began in 1981. Crested Butte is home to the Mountain Bike Hall of Fame, as well.

West Virginia can lay claim to popularizing what has become one of the sport's most legendary and imitated gatherings, the twenty-four-hour race. Begun in 1992 in Canaan, this through-the-night-with-lights event is one of off-roading's most grueling and popular tests. Teams of four or five riders compete, relay style, for a full day. Though each rider generally competes for eight hours, the race's bitter weather and highly technical trails hammer away cruelly at racers, especially in the cold, dark hours after midnight. Canaan has its roots in an early-season off-road event, Colorado's Leadville 100, as well as the Swiss Grand Raid Cristalp, an eighty-mile thrash that gains fourteen thousand feet and attracts four thousand riders—along with thirty thousand spectators—each year. The Canaan race itself is being duplicated by other full-day relays, including one outside Moab, where riders have the added misery of frequent snow falling on the course.

New off-road meccas are springing up everywhere. Mérida, Venezuela, is rapidly becoming the Durango of South America, or at least one of the many towns across that continent laying claim to the title. With hundreds of miles of relatively unexplored trails and a college-town-like atmosphere, Mérida, a two-hour flight from Miami, qualifies as a major off-road paradise. Its most legendary ride is a hundred-mile route that drops from the 14,500 foot Mifafi Pass to the town of Torondoy, near sea level. Other candidates for the South American Durango include Puerto Varas, Chile, gateway to both the Andes and Patagonia, and Peru's Cuzco, launching point for the Inca Trail and Machu Picchu. A Caribbean attempt to create an off-road paradise failed unexpectedly. Montserrat's first off-road festival was a success, but the entire island was overrun by lava the following year. No off-road technology has yet bested molten earth.

The Inca Trail, Peru.

ONCE A RIDER
SETS WHEEL TO A
TRAIL AND TELLS
A FEW FRIENDS, A
PLACE'S LEGEND
IS BORN. THIS IS
NOT TOO
DIFFERENT FROM
THE WAY FISHING
HOLES ARE
DISCOVERED.

Costa Rica is in a class by itself as an off-road destination. The country has always been a shredder's paradise, attracting ex-pat surfers, hikers, horseback riders, and river runners. The country is now actively appealing to mountain bikers, too, with several resorts, like the Turrialba Lodge, that model themselves after West Virginia's Elk River.

Ready for elevation to off-road-paradise status is Mexico. Copper Canyon, just a few hours from El Paso, Texas, truly ranks as one of the continent's most vast and challenging mountain bike destinations, with over ten thousand square miles of pure wilderness and hundreds of miles of trails. A Mexican off-road community has also emerged in Valle de Bravo, two hours southwest of Mexico City. Several pro bike shops there cater to a growing community of locals.

As people ride more and more places, trail access becomes a more widespread issue. In the United States, the tug of war between hikers, equestrians, and mountain bikers has gone on for over a decade, with singletrack as the flashpoint. Dozens of famous trails have been closed to riders in recent years in favor of walk-only use. The International Mountain Bike Association (IMBA) is spearheading efforts to reopen shutdown routes and to instill in riders the important ethic of low-impact riding. Trail-building days have become a tradition for many off-road communities. Some are modeled after Southern California's annual Mount Wilson Pancake Breakfast, where two hundred hard-working activists gather to labor intensely on their local trails.

While these are some of the most famous destinations and events in the off-road world, they are by no means the most popular. Those are the local trails and parks where everyday riders squeeze in their miles after work and on weekends. Some have attained legendary status: Mt. Tam, the Santa Monica Mountains outside Los Angeles, and Boston's Middlesex Fells. What these trails have in common is that they are user-friendly, close to urban areas, and fun. The unsung trails are, in a way, more important than the famous ones. They are the places where real mountain bikers—the ones who end up visiting Moab, Durango, Copper Canyon, and the Silk Road—are born.

The International Mountain Bicycling Association

For some riders, hitting the trails may be just another day in the park. But according to Tim Blumenthal, executive director of the International Mountain Bicycling Association (IMBA), there is more you should be thinking about when your bike meets the dirt. The IMBA was formed in 1988 to address global concerns confronting mountain bikers, such as trail maintenance, responsible riding, user conflict, and land management.

IMBA advocates what it calls "20-20-20 vision." This represents the $20 it costs to join your local bicycling club and get involved on the community level; the $20 annual membership in IMBA, which will involve you in the sport's wider, unified movement; and the twenty hours of volunteer time every rider should commit to spending on trail maintenance, trash removal, or appearances at public hearings. "Mountain biking on public land is a privilege," says Blumenthal. "This kind of involvement is a small price to pay for the privilege of riding the trails."

Bikers today have to share access with hikers and equestrians, and trails near metropolitan areas are especially prone to overpopulation and user conflict. Crowded trails detract from everyone's experience, and are, as Blumenthal says, "nobody's friend." Cyclists frequently feel themselves scapegoated. "On a wet trail, a bicycle tire leaves a pretty distinctive mark. But whether that mark translates into greater erosion than a footprint or a horseshoe—I don't think so."

IMBA's role in the ongoing conflict is to work within the system. This boils down to improving the image of mountain bikers, both by educating bikers in environmentally low-impact riding and trail maintenance techniques, and by educating policy-makers and other trail users of the importance of accommodating bikers as acceptable, prolific, and permanent users of the trails.

Blumenthal says the progress so far is visible. "There's greater awareness of the Six Rules (see IMBA's Six Rules of the Trail, p. 132), and thousands of miles of trails have been built or reopened to bikes. Land managers are developing a more positive image of mountain bikers, and bikers are helping more with construction and clean-up."

The Tsali Trail in the Nantahala National Forest, located in western North Carolina, is an example of one way that land managers have avoided the difficulties of shared-use trails. By implementing a system where several miles of the looping trail are designated off-limits to cyclists on alternate days, hikers who don't wish to encounter bikers can have access to the trails without fear of a heated run-in. It also means that the bikers, who cover twice as much ground, have a curtailed range on which to ride. Blumenthal considers this type of system a "last resort," not to mention difficult to enforce and communicate.

IMBA's Rules of the Trail

1) RIDE ON OPEN TRAILS ONLY.

Respect trail and road closures (ask if you're not sure), avoid possible trespass on private land, obtain permits or other authorization as may be required. Federal and state wilderness areas are closed to cycling. The way you ride will influence trail management decisions and policies.

2) LEAVE NO TRACE.

Be sensitive to the dirt beneath you. Even on open (legal) trails, you should not ride under conditions where you will leave evidence of your passing, such as on certain soils after a rain. Recognize different types of soils and trail construction; practice low-impact cycling. This also means staying on existing trails and not creating new ones. Don't cut switch backs. Be sure to pack out at least as much as you pack in.

3) CONTROL YOUR BICYCLE!

Inattention for even a second can cause problems. Obey all bicycle speed regulations and recommendations.

4) ALWAYS YIELD TRAIL.

Make known your approach well in advance. A friendly greeting or bell is considerate and works well; don't startle others. Show your respect when passing by slowing to a walking pace or even stopping. Anticipate other trail users around corners or in blind spots.

5) NEVER SPOOK ANIMALS.

All animals are startled by an unannounced approach, a sudden movement, or a loud noise. This can be dangerous for you, others, and the animals. Give animals extra room and time to adjust to you. When passing horses use special care and follow directions from the horseback riders (ask if uncertain). Running cattle and disturbing wildlife is a serious offense. Leave gates as you found them, or as marked.

6) PLAN AHEAD.

Know your equipment, your ability, and the area in which you are riding—and prepare accordingly. Be self-sufficient at all times, keep your equipment in good repair, and carry necessary supplies for changes in weather and conditions. A well-executed trip is a satisfaction to you and not a burden or offense to others. Always wear a helmet and appropriate safety gear.

Future

Just as off-roading's past
has been a marriage of
technology and popular
culture, the sport's future
will combine mechanical
innovation with the
human spirit.

The Way of the Wheel

Just as off-roading's past has been a marriage of technology and popular culture, the sport's future will combine mechanical innovation with the human spirit. To glimpse the future of mountain biking, one must remember that many of the basic concepts now driving the sport were already underway by the turn of the twentieth century, then lay dormant for decades, only to resurface in the present modern era. As with any industry, mountain biking is cyclical. While function remains a constant, trends rage and fade. Everything returns. But when an idea comes back, it brings with it an expanded community that hardly resembles what it was before.

If the past is any indication of the future, the average value of a bike will continue to increase, meaning higher quality for a lower price. Innovations such as aluminum frames, dual suspension, and grip shifting, which were previously out of the reach of many riders, will become increasingly more trail-worthy and affordable.

Future bikes may diverge from the fairly linear development of the past two decades. Bikes of today are lighter, faster, and more expensive than their predecessors, but they also look a lot like they did when people first started riding. The results of the next design wave will be radically different, however, not only in terms of frame material and design, but in a revolutionary rethinking of components. Brakes and derailleurs will be replaced by more durable, efficient, and self-contained parts, such as disc brakes and internally geared hubs. New technologies will improve chains and cables, the weak links today in terms of maintenance and longevity. Hydraulics and air systems will be integrated into brakes, enclosed drive systems, and other components to

Concept bikes serve the same function for the bike industry that the haute couture runway shows do for the fashion industry. The ideas presented are often extremely eccentric and expensive, but often imbedded in the prototypes are innovations that eventually trickle down to the mainstream.

improve performance. Computer and electronics technologies could significantly impact shifting and braking systems as well. Spoked wheels will give way to molded technologies, holding tires that no longer go flat. And of course, technologies that were once cast aside will be reincarnated.

Encouraged by the energy and success of riders like Phelan, Giove, Furtado, Pezzo, and DeMattei, more women will enter the sport than ever before, professionals and recreationists alike. It's already happening. Missy Giove deserves special credit for this. Her pet project, Team Amazon, is working to bring women from all economic classes into off-roading. More and more bike companies are also recognizing off-roading women by adding gender-specific models and components to their lineups.

One need only look at America's changing demographics to predict that bikes will also get more comfortable. As the population ages, the stiff hardtails of the 1990s will give way to more skeleton-friendly dual suspension bikes. At the same time, bikes for younger riders will be adapted to suit even more extreme terrain and radical riding conditions than ever before. So we can anticipate changes in the realms of comfort and performance.

Just as mountain bikes opened up the backcountry to human-powered mechanical adventure, they have now inspired a number of new hybrid vehicles among such user-groups as skateboarders, skiers, and the disabled. Mountain boards, which look like giant, wheeled snowboards with outrigger wheels, are appearing frequently on the slopes. Downhill wheelchairs, once the province of specialty racers only, are entering mainstream biking. Mountain biking will continue to cross-pollinate other extreme activities.

With this in mind, we can expect more places to ride, but they will be private places,

The Shimano Air Lines Project 2000 is a new shifting system attempting to replace cables with compressed air. It could signal a new era in derailleur technology and an end to frayed cables.

where riders pay to play. Mountain bikers have won many environmental battles over the years, but that may merely be a narrow view. While they've earned the right to ride alongside hikers and equestrians, the total amount of space open to all outdoor recreationists—especially near cities—is declining. Ski areas and parks help to lessen the growing deficit by opening venues where riders are catered to and watched over. The positive side of this is better trails, maps, and food for off-road adventures. True solitude, however, will become more distant, rare, and precious.

One of the greatest aspects of off-road racing has been its egalitarianism. Anyone could enter the Cactus Cup, just like racing giant John Tomac. But as professional categories of mountain bike racing attract ever-larger purses, we can expect changes on the competitive horizon. Huge events will leave little room for the average rider, so the citizen classes will be pushed away from the weekends and more toward mid-week, which is not a feasible proposition for most people. The official off-road sanctioning organizations have their hands full with international, high-dollar competition, leaving the field open for a new kind of citizen racing that harks back to the weekend free-for-alls from the sport's early days that are half festival and half blood sport. Without a primary emphasis on spectator appeal, we may see a return to the popular long, single-loop courses that predominated the sport's early events, such as Whiskey Town.

Globalization is yet another dynamic that molds the nature of fat tire biking. The off-road boom that raced across the United States in the early 1990s has swept Europe and Japan, and it will continue to spread toward newly industrializing nations. Driving this is a simple principle. In most countries, cycling is a basic human activity. As bike-friendly nations like Mexico, China, and Brazil gain larger middle classes, commuters will become recreational riders who will figure out ways to get their bikes, costly or not, onto trails.

The prognosis for mountain biking is good, but there are considerable challenges. The biggest one is keeping trails open. And while the bicycle remains by far our most environmentally sound mode of transportation next to walking, devising ways to manufacture bikes that significantly reduce pollution and other ecological impacts represents another challenge. That isn't happening much these days, although powder-coat paint has almost universally replaced the more toxic epoxy-based older finishes. Communities and local governments also have ample room to improve the amounts of streets and lanes dedicated to cyclists, so that bikes can be maximized for everyday commuting purposes, especially to and from the trail. Finally, bikes need to become safer and more user-friendly, especially for beginners. Shimano admits that novices are still intimidated by shifting and braking. Solving that problem will require education as well as technological innovation.

While the bike will surely evolve, and along with it, the ways and places we ride, the activity remains constant. The bicycle endures as one of humanity's finest inventions; it transports us under our own power into nature deeper, faster, and as well as any other vehicle. That won't change. Mountain biking will always be with us.

MOUNTAIN BIKE HALL OF FAME

1988

Gary Fisher: Assembled MTB progenitor ('74-'76); co-founder of MountainBikes ('79) and NORBA

Charlie Kelly: Co-founder, Repack ('76), MountainBikes, NORBA; founder, *Fat Tire Flyer* ('79)

Joe Breeze: Built first modern mountain bikes (Breezer, '77); co-founder of NORBA ('83)

Tom Ritchey: Framebuilder and parts designer; built first frames for MountainBikes ('79-'83)

Charlie Cunningham: Parts designer and builder of the first aluminum MTB frames ('79)

Murdoch: Early Pearl Pass rider ('76) and founder of Crested Butte, Colorado's Fat Tire Bike Week

Steve Cook: Catalyst of Crested Butte as MTB mecca; shop owner, national racer, trail builder

Jacquie Phelan: Three-time NORBA National Champ ('83, '84, '85); founder of WOMBATS ['87]

Mike Sinyard: Produced first large-run mass-produced mountain bikes (Stumpjumper, '82)

Joe Murray: NORBA National Champion ('84, '85); Bike designer at Marin, Kona, and VooDoo

1989

Erik Koski: First MTB mail-order business; Trailmaster bikes ('80)

Wende Cragg: Racer, early MTB photographer, first "Queen of Clunking"

Victor Vincente: MTB bike builder (Topanga, '79); racer and promoter

Jeff Lindsay: MTB framebuilder (Mountain Goat, '79)

Don Cook: Catalyst of Crested Butte as MTB mecca; shop owner, national racer, trail builder

Steve Potts: Framebuilder and parts designer, Wilderness Trail Bikes co-founder ('83)

1990

Scot Nicol: MTB framebuilder, Ibis Cycles ('82)

Tom Hillard: Race promoter, race official, co-founder of NORBA ('83)

Chris Chance: Early East Coast bike builder (Fat Chance, '83)

Glen Odell: Took over NORBA in '83 and made it thrive nationally for MTB racing and access

Cindy Whitehead: NORBA National Champ ('86, '90 [DH]); had legendary 49-mile seatless win

Ned Overend: NORBA National Champ ('86, '87, '89, ['90, '91, '92][and World Champion ('90])

*[ ] indicate achievements after inducted to Hall of Fame.

1991

Chuck "Bodfish" Elliot: Organized first off-road cycling race (Bidwell Bump,Chico, CA, '76)

Craig and Gary Cook: Builders of Cook Bros. Racing BMX-style MTB forks ('77) and frames ('78)

Mike Rust: Early Colorado MTB enthusiast, frame and parts designer and builder

Ross Shafer: MTB framebuilder, Salsa Cycles ('82); MTB parts designer and builder

Carole Bauer-Romanik: Catalyst of Crested Butte as MTB mecca; MTB Hall-of-Fame founder ('88)

John Tomac: NORBA National Champ ('88) Grundig World Cup ('91); World Champion ('91)

Al Farrell: MTB benefactor; helped NORBA, IMBA, and many in their early days and beyond

1992

Fred Wolf: Co-founder of Repack downhill races, Fairfax, California ('76); early bike tester

Tom Mayer: Early MTB enthusiast in Colorado; MTB parts designer

Mark Slate: MTB frame and parts designer, builder, Wilderness Trail Bikes ('83)

Gary Klein: Popularized use of aluminum for MTB frames ('84)

Ed Zink: Racing promoter; Iron Horse MTB Classics, World Championships (Durango '90)

Sara Ballantyne: NORBA National Champ ('88 [DH], '89); Grundig World Cup Champ ('90, '91)

1993

Otis Guy: Early clunker rider and Repack racer; designer, builder, racer (Otis Guy Cycles, '83)

Jimmy Deaton: Contender in big X-C and DH races for over a decade, from Repack to Kaprun

Gary Helfrich: Father of the titanium mountain bike; co-founder of Merlin; metals wizard

Alan Armstrong: MTB trail advocate; formed Mt. Wilson Bike Assoc. in Southern California ('85)

Don Douglass: Race promoter; co-founder of trail advocate group, IMBA ('88)

Charlie Litsky: Race promoter and announcer

Juliana Furtado: NORBA National Champ ('91, '92, ['93, '94, '95]); [Grundig World Cup ('93, '94, '95); World Champ] ('90, '92 [DH])

1994

Ignaz Schwinn and Frank W. Schwinn: Founder (and son) of Schwinn bike company (1895); popularized 26 x 2.125" balloon tire ('30s). They gave mountain biking its all-important tire.

Keith Bontrager: Parts designer ('84) and framebuilder, Bontrager Cycles; bench testing expert

Bill Cockroft: Designer of first MTB park, Mammouth Mtn., Calif.; introduced many DH races

Douglas Bradbury: Framebuilder (Manitou, '88); designer of suspension forks ('91), frames ('92)

1995

Richard Cunningham: Bike designer/builder (Mantis Bikes '81); Editor, *Mtn. Bike Action* ('93)

Junzo Kawai: SunTour parts maker; first large component company to recognize MTB'ing ('80)

Zapata Espinoza: Editor, *Mtn. Bike Action* ('87-'93); editor, *Mtn. Bike* ('93 on)

Kay Peterson-Cook: Catalyst of Crested Butte as MTB mecca; director, Fat Tire Bike Week ('89)

Steve Ready: Interbike Trade Show producer and MTB benefactor

1996

The Cupertino Riders: Rode geared clunkers near San Jose, Calif. ('73); pollinated Marin ('74)

Kent Erikson: MTB frame and parts designer/builder (Moots, '79); YBB suspension design ('86)

Marilyn Price: Founder, Trips for Kids ('87); bicycle advocate/environmentalist

Greg Herbold: DH racer; NORBA Nat. Champ ('88, '89, '93); World Champ ('90); Shimano tester

1997

Mert Lawwill: Designed MTB bikes (Pro Cruiser, '79); rear & front suspension designs ('89, '91)

John Parker: MTB designer/builder (Yeti Cycles, '85); many top racers started on the Yeti team

Susan DeMattei: Top three, NORBA National Series ('89-'96); Olympic bronze medalist ('96)

1998

Jim Hasenauer: Responsible mountain biking activist, co-founded CORBA, the Concerned Off-Road Bicyclists Association ('87), IMBA president ('91-'96)

Max Jones: Top racer, race promoter, U.S. National Team member ('90, '92)

Dean Crandall: Race official at mountain bike events worldwide, pioneered rules for USCF, NORBA and UCI's World Mountain Bike Championships

GLOSSARY

This Glossary was edited and compiled with permission from the Mountain Bike Almanac *and the* Internet Mountain Bike Slang Dictionary, *or* DIRTIONARY, *which was started by Jerry Dunn and maintained by Jim Frost. Contributors to the list include: Arlen Bankston, Jeff Deskins, Kelly Flannery, Alan Goldman, Catherine Heggtveit, Doug Landauer, Mike Landauer, Mike "Speed" Leska, Dave McSpaden, Mike Mitchell, Todd Ourston, Jeff Paul, Tom Purvis, Joshua Putnam, Mark "mojo" Radford, Matthew Silvia, and Rob Sutter. You can make your own additions to the list—and find revisions—at: http://world.std.com/~jimf/biking/slang.html*

air: Space between the tires and the ground. Both tires must be off the ground or it isn't "air."

ATB: All-Terrain Bike or Biking. A generic term for a mountain bike.

bacon: Scabs on a rider's knees, elbows, or other body parts.

bar end: Also known as climbing extensions, these bolt-on extensions provide additional, as well as more ergonomic, hand positions for climbing hills while the rider is raised up out of the saddle. *See* **hammering.**

bead: The portion of the tire that rests inside the box section of a clincher rim; it is pushed outward by the inflated inner tube, then held in place by the hooked lip of the rim's wall.

betty: Any female rider.

biff: A not-so-violent crash.

bonk: To run out of energy or grow exhausted on a ride. Also boink or **zonk.**

bottom bracket: Primary drivetrain component. The bearing mechanism with rotating axle that rests in the frame and is attached to the axle's right and left crank arms, allowing them to turn.

bottom out: To compress a shock absorber completely under a severe load or bump force.

brain bucket: Helmet.

brake pad: Rubber pad that stops the wheel by pressing against the rim.

braze-on: A fixture that has been welded, bonded or riveted onto the main frame or rear triangle to accommodate accessories such as water bottle cages, fenders, racks or cable guides.

bulletproof: A part or component that is virtually impervious to damage.

bunny hop: To lift both wheels off the ground by crouching down and then exploding upward, pulling the bike with you.

burrito: A rim braking surface that is bent inward toward the tube, forming a section that looks rolled, like a burrito.

butted: Term for a bicycle frame tube with a wall thickness that varies across its length.

cantilever brake: A simple, effective mountain bike braking system consisting of two vertical arms.

carbon fiber composite: Long, thin strands of carbon molecules that, when combined with a bonding matrix and compaction process, produce a material that possesses high strength, stiffness, and light weight.

carve: (From skiing.) To ride with great speed around the corners of a twisting fire road.

center to center: When measuring bike size, this refers to the measurement from the center of the bottom bracket spindle to the center of the top tube where it meets the seat tube, in a direct line from the bottom bracket spindle.

chainsuck: Condition when the bike chain gets jammed between the frame and the chain rings, or when the chainring is so worn that it holds onto the chain and lifts it up to meet the incoming part of the chain.

clipless pedal: Any pedal that uses a mechanical retention system in which the shoe is held in place by a cleat or claw. Called "clipless" because, in contrast to toe clips, you can't see the clips when you're clipped.

Clydesdale: A special racing class for riders over two hundred pounds (not officially recognized by NORBA).

corndog: To become covered in silt, usually after a fall.

crank arm: Primary drivetrain component that the pedals and chainrings are attached to, and which attach to the bottom bracket spindle.

dab: To put a foot down in order to catch your balance on a difficult section of trail. "I made it without crashing, but I had to dab once."

derailleur: Primary drivetrain component that moves the chain from one chainring or cog to the next.

dialed in: When a bike is set up nicely and everything works just right.

disc brake: A brake that uses a rotor and mechanically or hydraulically operated pads in a self-contained unit.

dual-track: A dirt road used by four-wheeled vehicles infrequently enough that their tires have made ruts that have become parallel singletracks. Also called doubletrack. *See* **singletrack.**

elastomer: Used primarily in suspension systems as the spring medium, it is a plastic material that is cast.

endo: The maneuver of flying unexpectedly over the handlebars, thus being forcibly ejected from the bike. In BMX riding, *endo* used to be a synonym for *front wheelie.*

ferrule: Outer cable end-cap that inserts into a frame's cable stop.

fire road: A wide, packed dirt trail (one to one-and-a-half vehicle width) that allows firefighting and ranger vehicles to access the back country.

forging: The formation of a component or part of a component by either pouring molten metal (aluminum, steel) into a mold (melt or warm forging), or stamping the material from a solid state via a high-pressure press into the desired shape (cold forging).

geometry: The combinations of vertical and horizontal angles and lengths of tubes that comprise the way a frame handles.

granny gear: The lowest gear available on a bike, one only a grandmother would need to use. It is designed for steep uphill climbing, but is extremely easy to pedal in on flat ground.

hammer: To ride fast and hard; a *hammerhead* is someone who hammers.

hardtail: Any bike with front suspension but no rear suspension. Contrast with rigid and full-suspension.

hike-a-bike: A section of a trail where the rider is forced to dismount and push the bike to maintain forward momentum.

hub: The component that allows the wheels to spin and to which the spokes are attached.

hybrid: A bicycle that combines the sturdiness, wide gear range, upright riding position, and secure controls of the mountain bike with the speed and reduced rolling resistance of a road bike's narrow tires and wheels.

IMBA: International Mountain Biking Association. An organization for trail advocacy.

line: The desirable path or strategy to take on a tricky trail section.

lug: A frame component that acts as a sleeve into which various tubes are inserted; a bonding process joins the lug and tube.

mojo: A charm or icon worn by a biker or attached to the bike.

monocoque: A term used to describe a one-piece molded frame.

MTB: The activity of mountain biking. Or a mountain bike itself: MTBing. *See* **ATB, OHV, ORV, VTT.**

mudsnake: Mud or moss covering a low-lying root or small dead-fall limb that lies diagonally across trails.

NORBA: National Off-Road Bicycling Association. Organizes most of the larger races in North America.

OHV, ORV: Acronyms for off-highway vehicle and off-road vehicle. These have motors and are not bicycles.

panniers: French term for saddle bags mounted on the front or rear of the bike.

peleton: A pack of racers riding together.

pinch flat: Also **snake bite**, it is the result of a tire hitting a sharp obstacle that in turn compresses the tube to the rim, pinching and cutting the inner tube in between, causing a loss of air.

pogo: To bounce on a full-suspension bike like a pogo stick. Also, for a full-suspension bike to bounce annoyingly and uncontrollably.

potato chip: A wheel that has been bent badly, but not as bad as a **taco**.

powerslide: A two-wheel sideways slide, with the foot opposite the direction of travel kept on the ground.

quick release: Also known as a "QR," this mechanism is used to hold a wheel's hub in the frame or fork's dropouts.

rebound: When the suspension system returns to its original position after being compressed.

retro-grouch: A rider who prefers an old bike with old components and isn't fond of new, high-tech equipment.

road rash: Large abrasions on a rider's legs and body caused by a crash, particularly on asphalt.

Shimano Pedaling Dynamics (SPD): The first successful mountain bike clipless pedal system. It uses a spring-laded mechanism much the same as a ski binding, to hold a cleat that is attached to the bottom of a cycling shoe onto the pedal.

singletrack: A trail just wide enough for one person or bike. Contrast with **dual-track**.

skid lid: Helmet. Same as **brain bucket**.

slick: A completely smooth or lightly grooved tire used primarily for maximizing a mountain bike's efficiency on asphalt.

snake bite: A double puncture of an inner tube, caused both by hitting an obstacle too hard and by under-inflation of tires. Also known as a **pinch flat**.

spider: The five-point star (four-point on Shimano's 1996 XTR) of the right crank-arm to which the chainrings are attached.

stiction: A combination of "static friction." The amount of initial friction a suspension unit possesses before the beginning of the compression stroke, and the force it takes to move the suspension.

suspension: Mechanism on the front and/or rear of the bike that reduces bump forces transmitted from the ground through the tires.

swag: The stuff that manufacturers and vendors donate to be given away at bike related events. Sometimes called *schwag*.

taco: To bend a wheel over on itself, in the shape of a taco. Worse than a **potato chip**.

technical: A section of trail that is difficult to ride because of rocks, tree roots, and steep drops.

threadless: A term associated with a Dia-Compe AheadSet headset or a similarly licensed headset that uses a system of a steer tube with no threads to connect the headset to the main frame's headset.

ti: Titanium. Some riders would replace their watches, rings, glasses frames, and gold tooth fillings with titanium if they could afford to.

toe clips: A clip-and-strap system that connects a rider's feet and toes to the pedals. Toe clips usually don't require special shoes.

tricked out: When a bike has the latest and hottest components.

VTT: *Vélo tout-terrain*, the French term for mountain biking.

washboard: Small, regular undulations of the soil surface that make for a very rough ride.

wash out: To have the front tire lose traction, especially while going around a corner.

winky: A reflector.

WOMBATS: Women's Mountain Biking And Tea Society, a Marin-based organization founded by writer and former MTB racer Jacquie Phelan.

The Zone: A state of mind experienced while riding.

zonk: Same as **bonk**.

Photography Acknowledgments

Copyright for individual photographs, as indicated below, is retained by the individual photographer.

Table of Contents/Foreword
Jeffrey Kausch — Table of Contents/Foreword (background)
Courtesy of Joe Breeze — Page 5 (left)

History
Wende Cragg — Pages 12-17, 21, 24, 25, 27, 72
Dave Epperson — Pages 18, 26
Courtesy of Charlie Cunningham — Page 29
Courtesy of Specialized Bicycles — Page 30

Technology
Roberto Carra — Pages 33, 34-35, 39, 47, 50-51, 52 (bottom), 53, 56, 58-59, 61 (bottom left), 62, 65 (left), 66-67, 68
Jeffrey Kausch — Page 43
Mark Dawson — Page 61 (top)
Dirk Belling — Page 45 (top)
Courtesy of Cannondale — Pages 36-37, 46, 52 (left)
Courtesy of Yeti Cycles — Page 40
Courtesy of RockShox — Pages 45 (bottom), 46 (left/far right), 52, 60
Courtesy of Amici Design — Pages 38, 41
Courtesy of Shimano USA — Pages 48-49
Courtesy of Spinnergy — Page 54
Courtesy of Mavic — Pages 55, 57
Courtesy of Syncros — Pages 63, 65 (right)
Courtesy of Chris King — Page 64

Culture
Jeffrey Kausch — Pages 69 (background), 71, 75, 83, 89, 94 (right), 95 (right), 97, 100, 106, 110 (left)
Matt Lanning — Pages 72 (left), 79, 103, 108, 109
Mark Dawson — Pages 72 (right), 81, 84, 85 (top), 104, 111
Jason Houston — Pages 80, 88
Markham Johnson — Page 86
Bob Allen — Page 87
Gabe Foo — Page 85 (bottom)
Zap Espinoza — Pages 93, 110 (right)
Jake Huffman — Page 90
Liz Steketee — Page 95 (left)
Kenny Brown — Page 98
Tom Evans — Page 112
SGT. Pete Thoshinsky, SFPD — Page 76 (bottom)
Courtesy of Swobo — Page 94 (left/top)
Courtesy of Berkeley Police Department — Page 76 (top)

Destinations
Melissa Muszynski — Page 113
Jeffrey Kausch — Pages 115, 132-133
Dave Reddick — Page 118
Markham Johnson — Page 120
Bob Allen — Pages 123, 127, 128
Markham Johnson — Page 124
Courtesy of BeachWay Press (all maps) — Pages 114, 116, 122

Future
Markham Johnson — Pages 134, 144
Courtesy of Specialized Bicycles — Page 135
Courtesy of Shimano USA — Page 136

Photographer Contacts

Bob Allen
Bob Allen Photography
P.O. Box 6219
Bozeman, MT 59771
phone/fax 406.388.7232
e-mail montanabob@mcn.net

Beachway Press Publishing
P.O. Box 5981
Glen Allen, VA 23058-5981
www http://www.beachway.com
e-mail scotta@beachway.com

Wende Cragg
Wende Cragg/Rolling Dinosaur Archives
12 Park Lane
Fairfax, CA 94930
phone 415.453.6762
e-mail JBleaux@aol.com

Mark Dawson/Matt Lanning
Fat Tire Fotos
530 Hampshire #305
San Francisco, CA 94110
phone 415.626.3278
fax 415.626.0109
e-mail fattireca@aol.com

Markham Johnson
P.O. Box 580
Tiburon, CA 94920
phone 415.435.6715
fax 415.435.6716
www http://www.mojofoto.com

Jeffrey Kausch
Jeffrey Kausch Photography
15-B Locke Lane
Mill Valley, CA 94941
phone 415.381.3794
fax 415.381.0817
e-mail jkausch@earthlink.net

David Reddick
P.O. Box 3553
Dana Point, CA 92629
phone 949.498.4168
e-mail dreddick@surferpub.com

Liz Steketee
2170 Harrison #2
San Francisco, CA 94110
phone 415.255.8373
fax 415.255.8321
e-mail stek@sirius.com

Amici Design is the brainchild of designer Lee Jakobs, a multidisciplinary creative studio that brings together a host of diverse talents. For the past nine years, Lee has collaborated with photographer/graphic designer Roberto Carra and writer/editor Dan Imhoff on a number of projects. They decided to create *Fat Tire* to celebrate the spirit of the sport of mountain biking, and to salute the bicycle, one of the greatest outlets for human ingenuity ever devised.

To Doug, the two Matts, Renee, Chris, Allison, Jan, the Sycip's, and all who have inspired this book and made sure I realize why this subject matter is as fun as it is.

Special thanks to Roberto Carra for continued inspiration and knowledge.

To Bo, my biggest supporter.

And, to Mom.

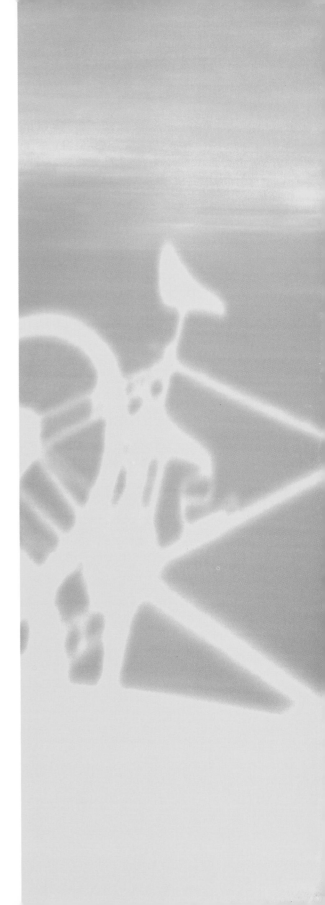